Memories

of

Bristol

Part of the

Memories

series

*The Publishers would like to thank the following companies for supporting
the production of this book*

Main Sponsor
MM Group Limited

Averys of Bristol Limited
BCWA Healthcare
Bristol Metal Spraying & Protective Coatings Limited
Bristol & West plc
Bristol Uniforms Limited
Bristol Water plc
Chappell & Matthews
HJ Chard & Sons
Clist & Rattle Limited
Fords Design Group Limited
The Galleries Shopping Centre
Great Mills (Retail) Limited
John Hodgson Distribution Limited
Imperial Tobacco Limited
Kemp Brothers Jewellers Limited
GF Mercer
Premier Transport
Redland High School for Girls
St Christopher's School
St Mary's Hospital
Charles Saunders Limited
Young, Humphrys & Lodge Limited

First published in Great Britain by True North Books Limited
Units 3 - 5 Heathfield Industrial Park
Elland West Yorkshire
HX5 9AE
Tel. 01422 377977
© Copyright: True North Books Limited 1999

ISBN 1 900463 78 4

Text, design and origination by True North Books Limited
Printed and bound by The Amadeus Press Limited

Memories are made of this

Memories. We all have them; some good, some bad, but our memories of the city we grew up in are usually tucked away in a very special place in our minds. The best are usually connected with our childhood and youth, when we longed to be grown up and paid no attention to adults who told us to enjoy being young, as these were the best years of our lives. We look back now and realise that they were right.

So many memories - perhaps of the war and rationing, perhaps of parades, celebrations and Royal visits. And so many changes; one-way traffic systems and pedestrianisation. New trends in shopping led that to the very first self-serve stores being opened.

Through the bad times and the good, however, Bristol not only survived but prospered. We have only to look at the city as it is today, with its finest remaining buildings now restored to their full glory, and the traditional tourist attractions now complemented by up-to-the-minute facilities, to see what progress has been realised and what achievements have been made over the last 50 years. Bristol has a history to be proud of - but more importantly, a great future to look forward to, into the new millennium and beyond.

Contents

Events & occasions

Reece Winstone Archive

It was 1937, and Wine Street along with the rest of the streets of Bristol saw rare scenes of gaiety when the new king was crowned. Floodlighting was used for the first time, to the amazement and wonder of Bristolians - especially the children - and Union Jacks and bunting, garlands and flowers, crowns and banners changed the city streets into a fairy wonderland of red, white and blue to welcome George VI to the throne. Every building, from the poorest cottage to the Council House, was hung with as much coloured bunting as people could get their hands on. The banners, of course, read 'GR' instead of 'ER', but in spite of Edward's popularity King George was already

beginning to establish himself in the affections of the people of Britain. Shadows of the coming world war were yet to fall on the rejoicing city, but a mere three years on Wine Street would lie in ruins and little would be left of these buildings where shoppers are here seen browsing in peace beneath the coronation garlands. In 1940 the King himself visited Bristol to encourage those who were suffering in the Blitz - a visit that was much appreciated by local people.

Throughout the war the King and Queen with their two beautiful daughters lived and suffered with the people of Britain, showing great courage by staying on in England when they could have been evacuated to safety.

Above: The poor of Bristol - many of them unemployed - had much to thank the Prince of Wales for back in the early 1930s, when people were still suffering from years of national depression and long-lasting unemployment that had marked the previous decade. A national Unemployment Fund had been created in 1928 - the 'dole' of a pitiful sum that was barely enough to keep alive on, yet infuriating to the well-to-do who saw it as encouraging laziness. Unbelievably, unemployment benefits were actually cut by ten percent in 1931 and the hated 'Means Test' introduced to examine the personal circumstances of those applying for help. The Prince of Wales took a personal interest in the plight of the men who were out of work and their families who never had enough to eat. A man of compassion and humanity, the Prince helped to set up centres and settle-ment schemes that brought some relief to the poor, not only of Bristol but of other large cities nationwide.

Prince Edward visited Bristol on 6th November 1934, and this photograph captures some of the exuberance of the welcome he was given by Bristol families, many of whom would have benefited from his help. He succeeded to the throne on the death of his father George V in January 1936, and renounced the throne on 10th December the same year for the American divorcee Wallis Simpson, 'the woman I love'.

Right: 'Can I have a ride, Dad?' A seat on the elephant's swaying howdah, far above the ground, was one of the excitements to be looked forward to on a visit to Bristol Zoo. This photograph dates from 1936, and the name of this patient elephant is not known. Rosie, however, joined the zoo two years later, and thrilled every child who rode around the zoo on her back until she died in 1961.

When Clifton Zoo was opened in 1835, its founders had serious study and scientific research on their minds rather than amusement. They soon found themselves in financial difficulties, however, and they realised that the zoo's survival depended on finding commercial attractions that would entice the public to spend money there. They were nothing if not imaginative with some of the ideas they came up with; alongside the more ordinary pursuits such as boat-ing on the lake, roller skating in summer and ice skating in winter, open-air concerts, golf and tennis, croquet and archery, the more unusual amusements like penny-farthing bicycle races and balloon ascents added the icing to the cake and proved immensely popular. In 1859 a balloon ascent would have set you back a shilling, with a concert thrown in for good measure. In more recent years the BBC's Natural History Unit used Clifton Zoo in its films, featuring the popular presenter Johnny Morris, who died in 1999.

Reece Winstone Archive

Above: Bristol, never slow to recognise the opportunity to party, had pulled out all the stops to celebrate the coronation of King George VI, our present Queen's father, on 12th May 1936. Beneath the streamers, garlands and bunting that waved gaily in the breeze, the Official Souvenir Programme went on sale around the city for the grand sum of twopence - affordable even by the poorest families. How many of these programmes survive? The photograph, taken in Corn Street near the nails, shows some of the decorations that were hung everywhere in the city in celebration.

The date of the coronation had been fixed some time before, when King Edward VIII came to the throne. The date was the same - but the king was a different one. King Edward abdicated when British protocol insisted that he could not marry Wallis Simpson, who was

A glance at the 1930s

WHAT'S ON?

In this heyday of the cinema, horrified audiences were left gasping at the sight of Fay Wray in the clutches of the giant ape in the film 'King Kong', released in 1933. Very different but just as gripping was the gutsy 1939 American Civil War romance 'Gone with the Wind'. Gable's parting words, 'Frankly, my dear, I don't give a damn' went down in history.

GETTING AROUND

At the beginning of the decade many believed that the airship was the transport of the future. The R101 airship, however, loaded with thousands of cubic metres of hydrogen, crashed in France on its maiden flight in 1930. Forty-eight passengers and crew lost their lives. In 1937 the Hindenburg burst into flames - the entire disaster caught on camera and described by a distraught reporter. The days of the airship were numbered.

SPORTING CHANCE

The black American Jesse Owens won a brilliant four world records in the 1936 Olympic Games in Berlin, thumbing the nose to Adolph Hitler's dreams of Aryan superiority. In a petty display Hitler walked out of the stadium and 'took his bat home'; later he refused to have his photograph taken with the victorious Owens.

divorced, and his younger brother the Duke of York was obliged to step into his shoes.

The new King George VI, a shy family man, had never expected to take the throne, but he dutifully took up the reins of kingship, encouraged by his beautiful queen, today our much-loved Queen Mother, and went on to shepherd his country through the second world war and to become one of the most popular sovereigns in history.

YB 9713

Reece Winstone Archive

Left: Back in 1934 every child in Bristol knew that if you wanted to see the real Father Christmas, Brights store in Queen's Road was where you should go. Other shops had their Father Christmases too, of course, but they were just men dressed up in red coats, white beards and a pair of wellies. A huge crowd, mostly composed of children, turned out on the 24th November to give the old guy a noisy and enthusiastic welcome to Bristol. Christmas started later in those days of widespread poverty and unemployment; how many of these children woke up on Christmas morning to find little or nothing in the stocking they had hopefully left out the night before? In today's commercially-minded society, Christmas trees, coloured lights and elaborate decorations find their way into the shops around the end of September, along with the endless gifts we are expected to spend thousands of pounds on. We would not wish for a return to the poverty of the 1930s - but oh, for those simple, non-materialistic Christmases!

With Santa in his open-top motor car were Robinson Crusoe and Man Friday, suitably dressed for the British winter in warm skins and fur caps. Too much realism, it was felt, might be rather chilly. Defoe's character Robinson Crusoe was based on the real-life sailor Alexander Selkirk, who was marooned for five years on the uninhabited Más a Tierra Island.

Rescued by Bristol seaman Woodes Rogers, Selkirk arrived back in England in October 1711.

Above: It was an exciting day for everyone when cowboy superstar and stunt rider Tom Mix appeared in a variety show at the Hippodrome, and on 5th March 1939 crowds lined the streets of Bristol to catch a glimpse of the Hollywood hero, jostling for the best views. Many fans stood at upper windows to get a grandstand view, while children were the lucky ones, grabbing a seat on Dad's shoulders. Mix's film career had started with the early silent films and had continued with the advent of the 'talkies' - a feat which was unusual in itself, as many of the stars of the day did not survive the transition. His films were immensely popular, his dark good looks and daring deeds setting many a feminine heart beating a little faster. Before his rise to fame, Tom Mix was a deputy marshal in his home town of Dewey, and it was his undoubted skills as a daredevil horseman that brought him real and deserved acclaim. The Western gained popularity in the earliest days of the cinema, offering many imaginative story-lines to the film-maker. The age-old struggle between cowboys and 'Indians' was real grist to their mill, but outlaws, lynch mobs, stampeding cattle, gun-fighters, stage coaches and sheriffs good and bad all went into the pot to be turned into edge-of-the-seat viewing. Great stuff.

Below: The coronation gave everyone a chance to declare their loyalty to the Queen - and it was party time in Bristol. Garlands and banners were hung in windows, lines of bunting stretched across every street, and though the weather on the big day was inclined to be cool and rather damp, it didn't stop the children from enjoying their street parties. Judging by the piano and the stage that had been erected, a party was clearly planned for the residents of Dean Crescent in Bedminster. Their imaginative decoration of the street had been awarded second prize in the competition for the best-decorated street that was run by the Western Daily Press.

The pageantry of the coronation is well-remembered by those who were lucky enough to see the event on television; people who had no set of their own crowded into the parlours of their more fortunate neighbours. The sight of the new queen being anointed with oil and having the crown placed upon her head is one which few can forget. Many are not aware that the Queen's coronation dress was itself symbolic, being embroidered with the emblems of the Dominions - India, Canada, New Zealand and Australia. The news on the morning of the coronation carried other news that the world had been waiting for - New Zealander Edmund Hillary, with John Hunt and sherpa Tensing, had reached the summit of Everest. The Daily Express headline said it all: 'All this and Everest Too'.

Right: Union Jacks flutter from every child's hand as well as from the upper windows of the George and Dragon. And what was all the excitement about? Princess Elizabeth was coming to town! Great crowds lined the roadside to cheer the beautiful 24-year-old as the royal car was driven through Bristol. The day might have been grey and overcast but the welcome given to the young princess more than made up for the darkness of the clouds overhead. Every available space was taken up by people clamouring to see their future Queen, taking up not only the pavements but upper windows, fences, balconies, steps, scaffolding and even the bonnets of cars. Rooftops, too, were fair game if a way could be found to get up there, and the roofs of the brewery in Old Market Street, the Victoria Rooms and the Drill Hall were filled with people who were determined to get a bird's eye view of the procession - though they would have missed seeing the Princess's smiling face as she drove by. What a reception Bristol gave her! The entire route was alive with flowers and flags; girl guides, school children, senior citizens, telegraph boys and Red Maids waved their hats, Union Jacks, handkerchiefs, streamers, rattles, and anything else they could get hold of, and enthusiastic students dressed in Elizabethan costume formed a tableau beneath the word 'Gloriana'. All this would, of course, have been part of a day's work to Princess Elizabeth; perhaps the Sheriff's car taking a wrong turning gave her a few moments' inward merriment....

Reece Winstone Archive

A glance at the 1930s

HOT OFF THE PRESS
The years of the 1930s saw Adolph Hitler's sickening anti-Jewish campaign echoed in the streets of Britain. On 19th October 1936 Oswald Mosley's 7,000-strong British Union of Fascists clashed head on with thousands of Jews and Communists in London, resulting in 80 people being injured in the ensuing battle. Mosley and his 'blackshirts' later rampaged through the streets beating up Jews and smashing the windows of their businesses.
A dark day in our country's history.

THE WORLD AT LARGE
In India, Gandhi's peaceful protests against British rule were gathering momentum. The Salt Laws were a great bone of contention: forced to buy salt from the British government, thousands of protestors marched to the salt works, intending to take it over in the name of the Indian people. Policemen and guards attacked the marchers, but not one of them fought back. Gandhi, who earned for himself the name 'Mahatma' - Great Soul - was assassinated in 1948.

ROYAL WATCH
The talking point of the early 1930s was the affair of the Prince of Wales, who later became King Edward VIII, and American divorcee Wallis Simpson. Faced with a choice, Edward gave up his throne for 'the woman I love' and spent the remainder of his life in exile. Many supported him, though they might not have been as keen to do so if they had been aware of his Nazi sympathies, kept strictly under wraps at the time.

It was 1951; the Festival of Britain was in full swing, and Bristol as usual was not going to be left out when it came to a celebration. Flags and banners hung everywhere proclaiming the Festival and welcoming visitors to the city. One of these banners in the city centre reminds us 'Virtute et Industria' (virtue in work), and though here and there scars remained to remind Bristolians of the war years, the city was poised on the threshold of a new and, it was hoped, prosperous future.

Reece Winstone Archive

The Festival of Britain was staged to celebrate the original Festival of 1851. It was the brain-child of Prince Albert, Queen Victoria's consort, and the extravaganza, which promoted British achievements, was staged in the purpose-built Crystal Palace.

One hundred years on, several buildings were constructed to mark the Festival's centenary, including the prestigious Royal Festival Hall and an exciting structure called the Skylon, which rose 300 feet above the exhibition grounds; illuminated at night, the Skylon was visible for miles around. A vast Dome of Discovery, intended to be a visible sign of national achievement, was built. Britain had indeed achieved much - but as every Bristolian knew, there was some way to go before post-war prosperity was theirs, indeed some goods were to remain on ration for a further three years. The 3rd July 1954 was the day the nation had been waiting for; crowds of people who were sick and tired of coupons gathered in Trafalgar Square and joyfully tore up their much-hated ration books!

Reece Winstone Archive

Left: A fascinating photograph that raises more questions than it answers. A smartly dressed salesman has collared part of a bombed-out building in Fairfax Street to make himself a bob or two, though frustratingly we can't quite make out exactly what he was selling! Whatever it was, it was obviously entirely riveting, as every eye is directed on the demonstration (or whatever) while the photographer and his (or her) camera goes unnoticed. Interestingly, men both old and young are in the majority in this group, though a few ladies can be seen on the outskirts of the action. The preponderance of males makes it unlikely that the subject of the presentation has anything to do with domestic arrangements or fashion. Could this fast-talking trader perhaps be demonstrating an ingenious invention for removing condensation from windows or pet hairs from furniture? Slick-talking salesmen have always been around to charm the pennies and shillings from people's pockets, and whatever was on offer, a few fivers (or perhaps tenners?) appear to be in the process of being handed over by punters eager to part with their cash.

This photograph was taken in 1955, and the cars in the background reflect the year. Mature readers will remember the old Ford Popular - and those vacuum wipers that gave up the ghost when you speeded up and flogged away like mad when you took your foot off! This site is today occupied by the Galleries Shopping Centre.

Above: This massive crown was erected in the Centre Gardens to celebrate the Queen's coronation on 2nd June 1953. The elaborate decoration was a thing of beauty with its red 'velvet' and jewels, all set on a base of royal blue. But it was after nightfall that the crown came to brilliant life, when hundreds of coloured lights sparkled like gemstones in the darkness. The crown was later shipped off to Canada, and we are not aware of its eventual fate.

To many people, not just in Bristol but around the country, the coronation of Queen Elizabeth II signalled the beginning of a 'new Elizabethan age', and after seeing her resolutely taking on the responsibility of the crown we all immediately took the young and pretty new Queen to our hearts. The occasion even called for the writing of new songs; perhaps some readers will remember 'Let's all be new Elizabethans'?

Unlike her father King George VI, Princess Elizabeth had begun her training for the throne early, when Edward VIII's abdication in 1936 made her the heir presumptive to the throne. She was only 14 years old when she broadcast messages of encouragement to the children of war-torn Britain, and as the war progressed she gradually took on more and more public duties.

'Pick a Pye for Christmas' was the commercial message of these Father Christmases who paraded outside an electrical store in The Horsefair in December 1960. Parents might have been concerned about their children seeing two Santa Clauses together, but really they need not have worried. After all, these red-cloaked and white-bearded men were not giving but selling, and children are quick to recognise a fake when they see one! The goods these Santas had on offer were transistor radios - the latest thing in gifts in the 1960s. The popularity of these novel miniature radios spread like the 'flu, quickly becoming all the rage, and no self-respecting teenager would be seen without his or her faithful 'tranny'!

Pocket-sized transistor radios had been developed by the Japanese company Sony as early as 1952, though it took a few more years before they became available in Britain at a price that most people could afford. The Horsefair and Broadmead were central to the enormous changes that had been made in Bristol after the second world war. Many old buildings that survived the bombing raids fell victim to the redevelopment and road building schemes of the 1950s. Thankfully John Wesley's Chapel - the oldest Methodist building in the world - survived unscathed. Wesley, who preached the gospel to vast crowds during the 18th century, built the chapel in 1739.

Down by the riverside

The phasing out of Bristol's trams began in 1938, and removal of the lines was causing havoc at regular intervals around the city. Some cities, of course, simply covered them over with tarmac, but not Bristol, where the scrap metal value of the lines was recognised and appreciated.

When work began early in 1939 on taking up the tram lines on Bath Bridge, workmen's lorries took station in the middle of the road and long queues of traffic formed in either direction, as can be seen from this photograph, taken on 3rd March. Getting to work and back home again in the rush hour would have been the worst, with traffic stacked up along Temple Gate and Bath Road.

Those riders on two wheels rather than four definitely had the odds stacked in their favour! The cyclist on the left would today be likely to be wearing a helmet, an innovation undreamed of back in the 1930s - in fact the wearing of helmets would probably have been written off as unnecessary and perhaps even 'sissy'! How times (and attitudes) change!

As the volume of traffic increased year by year, Bath Bridge was found to be inadequate to meet the growing need for wide roads that kept the growing number of vehicles flowing smoothly around the city. The situation was vastly improved by the addition of a second bridge nearby.

Reece Winstone Archive

Why was it that ice cream always tasted better when we were young? This ice cream seller near the corner of St Augustine's Bridge was caught on camera in June 1935, and he has quite a queue of youngsters to deal with, all hungry for their special treat. Every child's eyes are on his hands as he places a wafer in his mould, adds a scoop of ice cream, spreads it out and places another wafer biscuit on top. Then with a quick flip of his wrist out will come the finished product, a perfectly shaped ice to make another child happy. Readers will perhaps remember these well-insulated ice cream barrows that were common around the city's streets before the purpose built modern vans. Today, it seems that wherever we live we cannot escape the jangling music that can be heard several

Reece Winstone Archive

times a day as the ice cream seller tours our streets. Today's kids have a wider choice, however, than these children had, as these up-to-date vans will provide them with ice lollies and cold drinks as well as several different kinds of ice cream...which brings us back to our first question. Fifty years from now, will tomorrow's adults swear that ice cream tasted far better when they were children?

A glance at the 1930s

MELODY MAKERS
Throughout the 1930s a young American trombonist called Glenn Miller was making his mark in the world of music. By 1939 the Glenn Miller sound was a clear leader in the field; his clean-cut, meticulously executed arrangements of numbers such as 'A String of Pearls' and 'Moonlight Serenade' brought him fame across the world as a big-band leader. During a flight to England from Paris in 1944 Miller's plane disappeared; no wreckage was ever found.

INVENTION AND TECHNOLOGY
With no driving tests or speed restrictions, 120,000 people were killed on the roads in Britain between the two world wars. In 1934 a Halifax man, Percy Shaw, invented a safety device destined to become familiar the world over: reflecting roadstuds. In dark or foggy conditions the studs that reflected light from the car's headlights kept traffic on the 'straight and narrow' and must over the years have saved many lives.

SCIENCE AND DISCOVERY
By observing the heavens, astronomers had long believed that there in the constellation of Gemini lay a new planet, so far undiscovered. They began to search for the elusive planet, and a special astronomical camera was built for the purpose. The planet Pluto was discovered by amateur astronomer Clyde Tombaugh in 1930, less than a year later.

Reece Winstone Archive

Both pictures: So much has over the years been sacrificed in the name of progress, and motor vehicles have been central to that progress. In the gentler days of the 1920s, noise from the city's vehicles involved little more than the rattle of wheels and the clopping of hooves, and the only traffic pollution could be put to good use on the land! Things were soon to change, however, and by the 1930s traffic congestion in the city of Bristol was becoming a real headache. In a city that stood at the junction of no fewer than 11 main roads, motorists were demanding more facilities; they needed garages for their petrol and repairs to their vehicles, they wanted space to park near the shops, banks and businesses, and they needed better and wider roads and bridges. The problem was acknowledged, though the creation of wider roads meant the demolition of many older properties, and in 1936 work began on cutting new roads across the city. In a dramatic move that was to change the appearance of the city centre for ever, plans were drawn up to cover in a stretch of the River Frome that from the 13th century had been a lively quay reaching into the city as far as Colston Avenue. Work began in 1936, though for months little appeared to be happening. Ships still tied up at St Augustine's Bridge, though their days were numbered. HMS Fortune and HMS Firedrake *(left)* saw the end of the line, and this photograph taken on 3rd July 1937 captured an important part of Bristol's history. By this time the Dublin shed had been demolished and the site used temporarily as a car park (though how the front row of cars escaped a ducking defies imagination!). By the following year the scheme to culvert the river was well underway *(above)*. Site huts are dotted here and there, while huge cranes dwarf the workmen.

Reece Winstone Archive

Things ancient and modern - and Brunel's beautiful Clifton Suspension Bridge contrasts strongly with the civil engineering schemes of a much later generation. Opened in 1965, the roads and bridges of the Cumberland Basin complex speeded the flow of traffic between Bristol and Weston via what was, at 860 tons, the largest swing bridge in Britain. Looking towards the city, the hallowed grounds of Bristol City Football Club lie just off the photograph to the right, while on the horizon lies the rather select area of Clifton Downs. At one time the fine residences of the landed gentry lay here; today sports fields, retirement homes and private schools are dotted about the downs. But for the last 150 years it has been Clifton Suspension Bridge - the jewel in Bristol's crown - that has made the city memorable in the minds of thousands of visitors to the city. Isambard Kingdom Brunel was incredibly only 24 years old when he

A glance at the 1940s

HOT OFF THE PRESS

At the end of World War II in 1945 the Allies had their first sight of the unspeakable horrors of the Nazi extermination camps they had only heard of until then. In January, 4,000 emaciated prisoners more dead than alive were liberated by the Russians from Auschwitz in Poland, where three million people, most of them Jews, were murdered. The following year 23 prominent Nazis faced justice at Nuremberg; 12 of them were sentenced to death for crimes against humanity.

THE WORLD AT LARGE

The desert area of Alamogordo in New Mexico was the scene of the first atomic bomb detonation on July 16, 1945. With an explosive power equal to more than 15,000 tons of TNT, the flash could be seen 100 miles away.
President Truman judged that the bomb could secure victory over Japan with far less loss of US lives than a conventional invasion, and on 6th August the first of the new weapons was dropped on Hiroshima. Around 80,000 people died.

ROYAL WATCH

By the end of World War II, the 19-year-old Princess Elizabeth and her distant cousin Lieutenant Philip Mountbatten RN were already in love. The King and Queen approved of Elizabeth's choice of husband, though they realised that she was rather young and had not mixed with many other young men. The engagement announcement was postponed until the Princess had spent four months on tour in Africa. The couple's wedding on 20th November 1947 was a glittering occasion - the first royal pageantry since before the war.

entered his design for a new bridge to span the Avon Gorge - and won the contract. Sadly he was never to see his beautiful creation as although the foundation stone was laid in 1831 construction work on the bridge did not begin until after his death in 1859. Though Brunel's engineering masterpieces were many, he was well-liked and respected by his workmen because he was never too proud to roll up his sleeves, pick up a shovel and work alongside them.

Wartime

In 1939 Britain's Prime Minister Neville Chamberlain had made his announcement to the waiting people of Britain that '...this country is at war with Germany.' Bristol, along with the rest of the country rolled up her sleeves and prepared for the inevitable. This war would be different from other wars. This time planes had the ability to fly further and carry a heavier load, and air raids were fully expected. Air raid shelters were obviously going to be needed, and shelters were built on open places across the town.

By the time war was declared an army of volunteers of both sexes had already been recruited to form an Air Raid Protection service. At first ARP personnel were unpaid volunteers but when war broke out in September 1939 they became paid staff. It was their job to patrol specified areas, making sure that no chinks of light broke the blackout restrictions, checking the safety of local residents, being alert for gas attacks, air raids and unexploded bombs. The exceptional work done by Air Raid Wardens in dealing with incendiaries, giving first aid to the injured, helping to rescue victims from their bombed-out properties, clearing away rubble, and a thousand and one other tasks became legendary; during the second world war nearly as many private citizens were killed as troops - and many of them were the gallant ARP wardens.

At the beginning of the war Sir Anthony Eden, Secretary of State for War, appealed in a radio broadcast for men between 17 and 65 to make up a new force, the Local Defence Volunteers, to guard vulnerable points from possible Nazi attack. Within a very short time the first men were putting their names down. At first the new force had to improvise; there were no weapons to spare and men had to rely on sticks, shotguns handed in by local people, and on sheer determination . Weapons and uniforms did not become available for several months.

In July the Local Defence Volunteers was renamed the Home Guard, and by the following year were a force to be reckoned with. Television programmes such as 'Dad's Army' have unfortunately associated the Home Guard with comedy, but in fact they performed much important work. The Guard posted sentries to watch for possible aircraft or parachute landings at likely spots such as disused acrodromes, golf courses on the outskirts of towns, local parks and racecourses. They manned anti-aircraft rocket guns, liaised with other units and with regular troops, set up communications and organised balloon barrages.

Other preparations were hastily made around the city. Place names and other identifying marks were obliterated to confuse the enemy about exactly where they were. Notices went up everywhere giving good advice to citizens on a number of issues. 'Keep Mum - she's not so dumb' warned people to take care what kind of information they passed on, as the person they were speaking to could be an enemy.

Older Bristolians will remember how difficult it was to find certain items in the shops during the war; combs, soap, cosmetics, hairgrips, elastic, buttons, zips - all were virtually impossible to buy as factories that once produced these items had been turned over to war work. Stockings were in short supply, and resourceful women resorted to colouring their legs with gravy browning or with a mixture of sand and water. Beetroot juice was found to be a good substitute for lipstick.

Clothes rationing was introduced in 1941, and everyone had 66 coupons per year. Eleven coupons would buy a dress, and sixteen were needed for a coat. The number of coupons was later reduced to 40 per person. People were required to save material where they could - ladies' hemlines went up considerably, and skirts were not allowed to have lots of pleats. Some found clever ways around the regulations by using materials that were not rationed. Blackout material could be embroidered and made into blouses or skirts, and dyed sugar sacks were turned into curtains.

Above: War had been declared, and every citizen of Britain, young and old, male and female, was called upon to put his or her back into the war effort. Those who did not go into military service of one kind or another worked in factories, dug for victory, gave up their aluminium baths and saucepans, joined organisations and aided in any way they could. These boys were not going to be left out; they might be too young to fight but while there were sandbags to be filled they were going to do their bit to protect their school building. Thousands of sandbags were used during World War II to protect the country and its beautiful civic buildings.

Left: A proud father poses for the camera with his latest arrival. The baby had not arrived from Mars, in fact the 'arrival' was not a baby at all, but an anti-gas attack suit which was compulsory for babies in the United Kingdom during the Second World War. An air pump at the side of the suit enabled anxious parents to replenish the supply of air to the precious package inside. It is said that most babies were less than enthusiastic abut the prospect of being encased in the suit - and who could blame them? The picture was taken in 1939. In the event there was never any gas attack on British soil during the course of the second world war.

A glance at the 1940s

WHAT'S ON?
In wartime Britain few families were without a wireless set. It was the most popular form of entertainment, and programmes such as ITMA, Music While You Work and Mrs Dale's Diary provided the people with an escape from the harsh realities of bombing raids and ration books. In 1946 the BBC introduced the Light Programme, the Home Service and the Third Programme, which gave audiences a wider choice of listening.

GETTING AROUND
October 1948 saw the production of Britain's first new car designs since before the war. The Morris Minor was destined for fame as one of the most popular family cars, while the four-wheel-drive Land Rover answered the need for a British-made off-road vehicle. The country was deeply in the red, however, because of overseas debts incurred during the war. The post-war export drive that followed meant that British drivers had a long wait for their own new car.

SPORTING CHANCE
American World Heavyweight Boxing Champion Joe Louis, who first took the title back in 1937, ruled the world of boxing during, making a name for himself during the 1940s as unbeatable. Time after time he successfully defended his title against all comers, finally retiring in 1948 after fighting an amazing 25 title bouts throughout his boxing career. Louis died in 1981 at the age of 67.

Reece Winstone Archive

Above: Rotted sandbags meant holes to push your fingers through and lots of nice trickly sand to play with and to scatter around the pavement - if you were five years old, that is! When war broke out in 1939 the filling of sandbags became a priority, and even older school children helped out in the work of filling the thousands of bags needed around the city. Young and old, men and women alike were called on to play their part in the war effort - even if it meant doing boring jobs like shovelling sand into bags! Sandbags were piled high around every important building and every ARP post in Bristol, protecting them from bomb blast. The British weather quickly told on the sandbags, however, and the hessian bags lasted only a matter of months. Piled up outside doors and windows, sandbags provided excellent cover from bomb blast and prevented windows shattering, and the owners of shops, offices, pubs and on occasions even private houses - like the one seen in this photograph - also resorted to sandbagging their premises. Other people stuck tape in criss-cross patterns across their windows or covered them with net - anything to prevent injury from flying glass in an air raid. Splinter-proof lacquer painted on windows was another favourite way to protect one's property.

Right: It was 8th May 1945, and Winston Churchill and President Truman had proclaimed VE Day. Out came the flags and the bunting, and this entire community in St Michael's Hill went wild with joy when the news that everybody was waiting for was announced. It was good to be alive; after all, so many were not, and along with the rest of Bristol these residents let their hair down and turned the event into a city-wide knees-up. A toddler gazes up in wonder at the hated Adolph Hitler, whose effigy has been suspended high above the street. Revenge, it is said, is sweet - but vengeance was not theirs; Hitler had already renounced his dream of a thousand-year Reich and had gone ahead to meet his maker. He and Eva Braun had committed suicide together just the week before, on 30th April. In the Pacific the war continued for a further four months; the Japanese surrendered on September 13th. When Bristol had had time to draw breath, there was much to be done to restore the city that had suffered such extensive bomb damage. Strange as it may seem, rebuilding started with demolition, and whole areas of the city were swept away in the name of progress. It is hardly surprising that many of the buildings that rose from the rubble were poorly designed. Housing was desperately needed, and new estates built in the 1950s included 15-storey blocks of flats, where few people from the old communities felt at home.

Soon after the outbreak of war in 1939, people were preparing for the worst. They learned how to put on their gas masks, grow vegetables in their flower gardens, give first aid and fight fires. Volunteers of both sexes were urgently needed to fulfil all kinds of duties; Air Raid Precaution wardens were appointed, and men who were outside the age for military service joined the Home Guard. The Women's Land Army, the evacuation service, the Women's Voluntary Service and the Auxiliary Fire Service all sought recruits, and the men and women of Bristol pulled their weight. Watched by a group of children who, it is hoped, did not go home soaked to the skin, these auxiliary firemen are practising their new skills in Stapleton Quarry. Their expertise was to be

desperately needed during the horrific scenes of devastation that reduced huge areas of our city to rubble. The National Fire Service took on the control of all civic fire brigades during World War II, and women as well as men worked for the NFS. Was their role merely supportive, or did they play an active part in fighting fires? Many women certainly acted as fire watchers; on occasions incendiaries fell into unattended office blocks and factories and started fires, many of them burning unchecked in city centre properties. Firewatching eventually became a compulsory duty, and all men between 16 and 60 were called on to organise a fire-watching rota. Later on women between 20 and 45 joined them.

Reece Winstone Archive

Below: *It was April 1940, and though at home little appeared to be happening and people were talking about the 'phoney war', in Scandinavia things were hotting up and the war was far from phoney. Russia was invading Finland and Germany was planning a full scale invasion of Norway and Denmark (which was geographically in their way). Hitler was more than slightly miffed when ten of his destroyers, a heavy cruiser and a couple of light cruisers were all sunk, and other vessels badly damaged, an event that made headline news.*
This newspaper seller had no way of knowing that seven months on war would have become a grim reality for everyone in Bristol, and that his patch on the corner of High Street and Wine Street was destined to disappear in the onslaught of enemy bombs. The Dutch House, seen in the background of this nostalgic photograph, was bombed on 24th November. How many readers will remember the well known larger than life tin soldier that used to stand on the balcony? He was rescued from the ruins and given a place in the City Museum. The Dutch House, reputed to have been built in 1676 as a merchant's residence, had become by the 1920s and 30s the premises of the Irish Linen and Hosiery Association, one of the city's favourite drapers shops. By 6th December the building had been demolished and in later years a branch of the Bank of England was built on the site.

Reece Winstone Archive

BELLS WILL NOT BE RUNG EXCEPT AS ALL CLEAR FOR GAS

DON'T LISTEN TO RUMOURS ASK US.

During World War II the public were bombarded with slogans that rained down on them as thickly as German bombs: 'Dig for victory!'; 'Britain can take it!'; 'Careless talk costs lives'; 'Make do and mend'. The posters that were designed to boost morale and keep people security conscious appeared on every available advertisement hoarding. Rumour could spread panic like wildfire and was seen as a real danger, so the Air Raid Prevention wardens based in Brunswick Square decided to run a poster campaign of their own.

Even before war was declared an army of volunteer ARP wardens of both sexes was recruited, probably the largest percentage of them coming from the upper and middle classes. At first the ARP personnel were unpaid volunteers but when war broke out they became paid staff. Wardens were there first of all to give help and information, though their duties involved a thousand and one other tasks. They made sure that blackout restrictions were kept and checked the safety of local residents, ever on the alert for gas attacks, air raids and unexploded bombs. When the bombing began in earnest they dealt with incendiaries, gave first aid to the injured, helped to rescue victims from their bombed-out properties and cleared away rubble. During the war nearly as many private citizens were killed as troops; sadly many of them were ARP wardens.

Reece Winstone Archive

Reece Winstone Archive

Above: A lot of information in a nutshell: three terse notices on the windscreen of this car inform us that this driver is deaf, he is willing to give lifts to service men - and that his tax expires at the end of December 1940, pinpointing the year of the photograph for us.
In wartime it was vital to advertise the fact that you suffered from a disability such as deafness, as slowness to understand a question or obey a command would certainly incite suspicion from a police officer, an ARP warden or a Home Guard patrol. How else would they know at a glance that he was not a German spy who could neither understand nor speak English? No innocent and harmless British driver going about his own business wanted to spend the night behind bars under suspicion of being a German infiltrator or a fifth columnist! The service of offering lifts to soldiers, sailors and airmen must have been very much valued by men on leave (women were even then all too aware of the dangers of hitch-hiking). A lift back to the camp after a night out in town would have been appreciated, while service men who had a weekend pass often hitch-hiked in preference to waiting around for buses, trams and trains. When they wanted to go home to see their families, hitch-hiking was usually far faster in the end.

Top: An all too common sight during the second world war - homes reduced to a pile of rubble by Nazi bombs, and families made homeless. This row of four houses in St Agnes Avenue suffered extensive damage in the blitz that wiped out many of Bristol's buildings on Good Friday 1941. People rescued what few pitiful belongings they could, and descended where possible on their relatives. Relatives, too, might have found themselves homeless however, and many bombed out families in Bristol had to find a temporary home in tents. Drivers who needed to go through the city grew used to roads being completely blocked to traffic, and picking one's way around the huge piles of rubble was commonplace, whether you drove a bus or rode a push bike.

Readers with a sharp eye might pick out the barrage balloon on the left, flying in nearby Victoria Park. As soon as an air raid siren sounded it was time to fly the barrage balloons that had been placed in the most important areas around the city. Parks, recreation grounds, private land, tips, sites cleared for building, and plots of unoccupied land were the obvious choice. When flying high over the city (the maximum flying height of the balloons was 6,000 ft), this ingenious form of defence prevented enemy planes from diving low over the streets to make close-up attacks.

A glance at the 1940s

MELODY MAKERS
The songs of radio personalities such as Bing Crosby and Vera Lynn were whistled, sung and hummed everywhere during the 1940s. The 'forces' sweetheart' brought hope to war-torn Britain with 'When the Lights go on Again', while the popular crooner's 'White Christmas' is still played around Christmas time even today. Who can forget songs like 'People Will Say we're in Love', 'Don't Fence Me In', 'Zip-a-dee-doo-dah', and 'Riders in the Sky'?

INVENTION AND TECHNOLOGY
Inspired by quick-drying printers' ink, in 1945 Hungarian journalist Laszlo Biro developed a ballpoint pen which released viscous ink from its own reservoir as the writer moved the pen across the page. An American inventor was working on a similar idea at the same time, but it was Biro's name that stuck. A few years later Baron Bich developed a low cost version of the pen, and the 'Bic' ballpoint went on sale in France in 1953.

SCIENCE AND DISCOVERY
In 1943 Ukrainian-born biochemist Selman Abraham Waksman made a significant discovery. While studying organisms found in soil he discovered an antibiotic (a name Waksman himself coined) which was later found to be the very first effective treatment for tuberculosis. A major killer for thousands of years, even the writings of the ancient Egyptians contain stories of people suffering from tuberculosis. Waksman's development of streptomycin brought him the 1952 Nobel Prize for Medicine.

Below: Everyone loves a parade, especially when it is headed up by a band playing a rousing march, and huge crowds lined the streets of Bristol to watch this American regiment march down Park Street. They were no doubt delighted with the style of the American marching band, which has traditionally been seen as being rather more flamboyant than the British. US soldiers were a familiar sight in the city; Clifton College, for example, was vacated during the war and the whole school evacuated to Bude, and American troops occupied the buildings from 1942. The presence of so many 'Yanks' in the city had another effect - many of the GIs based in Bristol formed relationships with local girls, who were delighted with the steady supply of dates and dancing partners! We have no firm date for this photograph, but the event is likely to have celebrated the end of the war, either on VE Day or perhaps VJ day on 20th August 1945. Could it perhaps have been part of the huge Thanksgiving Parade that was staged in Bristol to mark VJ day? Evidence of the wartime bombing raids can still be seen here on both sides of the roads. Thankfully the University Tower, seen in the background, survived. Built by the Wills family of tobacco fame as a memorial to their father H O Wills, the tower has been a familiar landmark in the city since it was completed in 1925.

Right: The war was over, and Bristolians were tired of bombs, gas masks, the blackout and all the other privations of wartime Britain, and when peace was declared after six long years of war bunting was strung from house to house across every street and patriotic flags flapped gaily in the breeze. Along with the rest of Britain they found the energy to let their hair down and organise Victory Parades, street parties, fireworks displays and bonfires. Huge crowds gathered outside the Council House along Corn Street to hear the Lord Mayor, Cllr W F Cottrell, officially declare that the war in Europe had ended.
He made the announcement from the historic coach which only rarely sees the light of day, being reserved for special occasions such as the accession of a monarch to the throne, a coronation - or the end of a war. It was Britain's new Prime Minister, Clement Attlee, who brought the nation down from its euphoria with a resounding bump. He gave the country a serious warning that although Britain was once more at peace, there was no likelihood of prosperity for the country in the immediate future. Across the world countries were decimated by war, and there were worldwide food shortages. It would be several more years before people could stop using tinned dried eggs or shop for clothes without counting how many coupons they had.

Reece Winstone Archive

A masterpiece of success in direct marketing

Andy Warhol, the famous 60s pop artist, once said, 'Being good in business is the most fascinating kind of art'. Whether or not you agree with this statement, nobody can fail to be fascinated by a success story about a talented artist who establishes a successful business empire. It is a true story; its heroine is a lady named Vera Hughes, the company she founded is the acclaimed Mail Marketing, and her talent for drawing and painting can be seen in the many pictures which hang on the walls of the company headquarters at Springfield House, where they brighten up the lives of staff and visitors.

associated with mailings which attracted a high level of interest - the postman must have been one of the first people to realise that the new business over the shoe shop was going to be a success! On one particularly fortuitous occasion, Mail Marketing was contracted to fulfil orders for a wild bird seed dispenser, sent in response to an offer on the back of bird seed packs. This might have turned out to be a fairly routine contract, but it so happened that the offer coincided with an unusually severe spell of winter weather, and great publicity was given by the media to the plight of the poor birds who were unable to find food because the

When Vera Hughes was still a young girl it was already plain that, if talent was any guarantee of success, Vera would be a very successful lady indeed; the only question-mark was over the direction which her success would take. Her first career ideas were frustrated through no fault of her own. Having studied art at Barnstaple College, she had gained experience in a number of commercial sectors, including fashion advertising. She was interested in fashion, and when she won the Prix de Paris for her dress design work it seemed that her future was settled. Unfortunately, this was at a time when Hitler's activities in Germany were causing repercussions across Europe, and the situation made it impossible for Vera to pursue this ambition any further. She then turned her attention towards developing a career in the print industry, but soon discovered that, although she was extremely well-qualified in graphic reproduction, the print industry was so male-dominated that there was little prospect of her finding an opening. With indomitable spirit, Vera then decided to explore the potential of the direct mail fulfilment business, and in 1950 she took on half a dozen staff and set up as Mail Marketing, in premises above a shoe shop in Park Street.

ground was frozen, and were starving to death as a result. The kind-hearted British public rose to the occasion and ordered wild bird seed dispensers in their thousands; stocks very soon ran out, so, to meet the unexpectedly high level of demand, the client ordered a very large number of dispensers from Sweden, and these were duly delivered to Mail Marketing's small office in Park Street. Vera and her staff were rather embarrassed when they arrived at work one morning to find that the pavement outside the office was impassable because it was completely blocked by stacks of boxes of bird seed dispensers. However, they quickly recovered

Top: *Vera Hughes, founder of the MM Group.*
Below: *Hand packing in the early days at Park Street, late 1950s.*

From small beginnings
Mail Marketing began in a modest way, concentrating on handling coupons but using these as a means of building up its own mailing list. From the very outset the company had a habit of being

Left: *The Clifton Wood factory in 1960.* **Below:** *The enclosing department.* **Bottom:** *Artist's impressions of Mail Marketing's various premises in and around Bristol in the 1960s and 1970s.*

projects which the company has been involved with - so far.

The company's commitment to setting high standards in every aspect of direct mail fulfilment is reflected in its involvement in the various industry bodies which have been set up. 1977 saw the formation of the Direct Marketing Association, with Vera's son John as one of its founder members. In 1988 the Direct Marketing Centre, which was to be the forerunner of the Institute of Direct Marketing,

from the shock and set about despatching the dispensers so that pedestrians could walk up and down Park Street again; work continued day and night until the backlog was cleared.

Thanks to the flair and determination of the business's founder and the hard work of her staff, combined with the occasional stroke of good fortune, or good timing, as in the case of the bird seed dispensers, Mail Marketing continued to grow. By the end of the decade the number of employees had risen to 30, and with business increasing all the time the staff's jobs and wages - 1s 9d an hour for hand packers - were assured. Throughout the 1960s expansion continued at a rapid rate. By 1965 the annual turnover had reached £60,000, and the Park Street office was no longer large enough to cope. The larger premises of Springfield House in Welsh Back were secured; since this time the company has retained the name of Springfield House for its headquarters. Mail Marketing's client list was by this time becoming impressive, and already included Realm Records, Forecourt Advertising Services (many readers will remember the excitement of collecting Shell Tokens for free drinks glasses in the early days of petrol promotions, back in 1968) and Fleur Mail Order, on whose behalf Mail Marketing sponsored a racing car, perhaps one of the most glamourous high-profile

was established, again with John Hughes of Mail Marketing as a founder member. The following year Mail Marketing was one of the first companies to join the Mailing Preference Service. In recent years the company decided to formalise its own

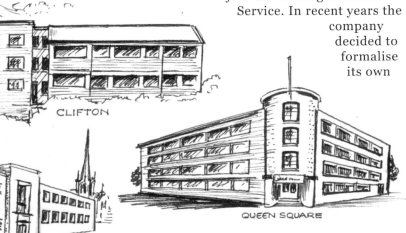

CLIFTON

REDCLIFFE

QUEEN SQUARE

internal quality auditing systems, and in 1996 obtained accreditation to the ISO 9002 quality standard.

By 1984 Mail Marketing's standing was such that it was invited to participate in handling the first flotation of BT shares. Having dealt successfully with this challenge, they were also made responsible for liaising with the public in the subsequent flotation of British Gas and TSB; and it was their experiences in handling the huge response to these flotations, with a significant number of enquirers choosing to respond by telephone rather than by mail, which led Mail Marketing to expand into telemarketing through the acquisition of the automated telemarketing bureau Mediaphone. Started as a small concern by two former BT employees in 1989 and purchased by Mail Marketing in 1992, the Mediaphone Call Centres today are operated by carefully-recruited and highly-trained staff working from three call centres, two in Bristol and one in Northern Ireland, and have invested in the latest technology which routes calls to the appropriate operator and provides on-screen help according to client requirements. The operators are involved with both inbound and outbound telemarketing - receiving and making calls - and provide a comprehensive and highly professional service to a wide range of clients. The variety of clients means that the nature of the work the Mail Marketing staff undertakes varies tremendously, from selling home delivery of papers for regional newspapers such as the Bristol Evening Post to handling requests for

literature on behalf of financial organisations and supplying information about a customer's existing investments. With consumers becoming increasingly phone-friendly, telemarketing is a definite growth area; the number of calls handled per year increased from three million in 1997 to five million in 1998, and this trend is expected to continue.

The current Chairman of the company is Vera's son, John Hughes, who joined the company in 1965, and has worked hard to keep Mail Marketing, now MM Group, amongst the leaders of the industry. His hard work has brought success

Top: *A selection of early printed material produced by Mail Marketing during the 1960s.*
Right: *The Princess Street premises in 1979.*

at both company and individual level; not only has MM Group flourished, but his efforts gained him personal recognition in 1987 when he won the prestigious Robert Bill Award, and again in 1998 when he won the Royal Mail Award for his contribution to the direct marketing industry. It has thus been clear for many years that John has inherited his mother's business talents, and we now have irrefutable evidence to prove that he has inherited

Left: *John Hughes, Vera Hughes and Trevor Perkins Financial Director (retired in 1999).*

her talents for drawing and painting as well. The company's Christmas card, which for many years was designed by Vera, became John's responsibility for the first time in 1998, and his irresistible design of Christmas teddy-bears not only carried compliments of the season to the company's clients, suppliers and associates, but also raised much-needed funds for the Jack and Jill Appeal to improve medical and nursing facilities for children at Frenchay Hospital.

An exciting venture launched in 1997 was Electronic Business Solutions, or MMEBS, which was set up to provide a bank of expertise and resources which would bring electronic commerce within reach of clients. Services included, then as now, the design and management of E-mail and Internet systems. This was an exciting area to be involved in as advanced technology was opening up tremendous

Above: *Springfield House, West Street pictured in the late 1990s.*

Above: The Company Christmas cards designed by Vera Hughes and, in 1998 by John Hughes. *Left: An Advantage automated inserted machine.* *Below: Springfield House today in West Street, Bedminster.*

It might seem that the original mailing activities of the firm have been to some extent overshadowed by the development of these highly advanced, hi-tech direct marketing tools, but this is not the case at all; mailshots remain a vital ingredient of marketing campaigns, and a significant proportion of responses continue to arrive by post. Mailing has of course benefited from the availability of increasingly sophisticated equipment. The methods used have evolved considerably since the days when a band of girls stuffed and addressed envelopes in the little office above the shoe shop. Beginning with moves towards higher levels of personalisation, techniques have continued to evolve to keep pace with customer expectations and increased volume. In the

opportunities to reach the new 24-hour global marketplace, and early clients included major international companies who wished to make sure they stayed at the forefront of developments. One of MMEBS's first fulfilment services was for Wallace and Gromit merchandise, and it is thanks to them that Wallace and Gromit fans the world over have been able to place electronic orders for items from T-shirts and baseball caps to fridge magnets and Christmas cards, while state-of-the-art encryption guarantees absolute security of their credit card number and other sensitive personal information. Now Enid Blyton fans can enjoy similar benefits; in addition to games, puzzles, information and a Mystery and Adventure Treasure Hunt with the Famous Five, the Enid Blyton website includes The Enid Blyton Store, created by MMEBS, where visitors can order any books and merchandise from the catalogue, plus a Noddy T-shirt which is exclusive to the site. MM Group is handling the fulfilment for all orders for Enid Blyton merchandise, and items are despatched all over the world, from stock held in the secure warehouse at the Bristol site, within 48 hours of receipt of order, whether by mail, telephone or via the Internet.

early days of computer usage, the simple inclusion of the addressee's name at the top of the letter made a mailshot stand out; now, recipients are no longer so easily impressed, having come to expect a high level of accuracy and personalisation within a mailing. Increasingly advanced equipment has been developed to incorporate each new sophistication and to permit higher volumes and greater complexity, such as the incorporation of illustrations, the use of larger format envelopes and the enclosure of promotional items such as pens and free sample sachets. One great step forward was the development of infra-red technology to produce Matched Mailers, which could handle multiple pages with up to 14 inserts and could even handle selective enclosing automatically. Today, MM Group operates many high tec. enclosing machines which output a total of 200 million filled envelopes per year. The personal service has not been completely superseded, however; sometimes customers still opt for mailings that are so complex that even today's machines cannot cope, and so the staff has not lost its hand enclosing skills - although they do expect considerably more than 1s 9d an hour for this service today.

With mail marketing, telemarketing and electronic marketing all representing powerful tools and offering companies a choice of media in which to advertise, planning a marketing strategy and laying out response channels have become immeasurably more complex operations than they were previously. In many cases an advertising campaign will be composed of a mix of the three options. In order to offer clients an integrated service, Mail Marketing, Mediaphone and Electronic Business Solutions have now consolidated to form MM Group. The new

structure means that campaigns being run simultaneously through different media can be handled in a totally seamless way, with postal, telephone and Internet responses integrated into a single response management service based on a sound knowledge of marketing and experience of every available strategy. Ian Hughes, son of John Hughes, sees the provision of a personal service to customers as a very important factor in the future. As he points out, 200 years ago people expected personal service from tradesmen; if they ordered a new suit from a tailor, they would expect that tailor to visit them at home, take their measurements, then go away, get to work, and come back later with a hand-made suit that fitted perfectly. In recent years people

Top left: *Old and New! Dark green vans reflect the updated MM Group image.* ***Below:*** *Ian Hughes with Gromit, one of MMEBS's first fulfilment services for Wallace and Gromit merchandise.*

have lost sight of this service to a great extent, patronising instead the retail chains and out-of-town shopping malls, but Ian Hughes is convinced that people are now returning to firms that can provide the personal service tailored to their own individual needs. This, then, is what the response services team is aiming to provide. If a customer is most comfortable with the Internet, they use the Internet; if a customer feels more at home with the telephone or the post, then that is the medium which is used; the customer's wishes are paramount. MM Group is able to do this because it has consistently been at the cutting edge of new marketing channels and so is able to cope with even the most unexpected of customer demands; it welcomes new challenges, seeing them as a way to constantly improve its service and remain competitive, and it is well placed to help customers make the most of the new marketing opportunities being opened up by the information superhighway as it breaks down trading barriers in the global market. It is interesting to note that Bristol which grew as a place of adventure and communication is utilising the internet and internet technology for the rebirth of the City's trading heritage.

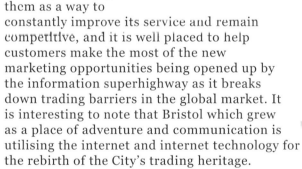

Another related area where MM Group has been quick to spot potential for development is in exploiting the Internet as a means of collecting donations to charities. Leading charities such as the RSPCA, Oxfam, Mencap and Shelter are longstanding users of MM Group's traditional services, with some 10 million donations being received on their behalf by post and telephone; however, very few charities had the facilities to accept donations over the Internet. In 1998 MM Group established Echarity, which gives millions of potential donors access to a range of charities through a single Internet address with donation pages specific to each charity which uses the service. MM Group deals with all aspects of the donation process, from designing the donation pages, which can be integrated with clients' own sites, to processing and auditing the transfer of

funds into the charity accounts, generating the thank-you e-mails and compiling donor e-mail lists. The Echarity web server is protected by a state-of-the-art firewall to prevent unauthorised access, and the latest encryption protocol conforms to the current Internet standard which MM Group was itself instrumental in developing.

Throughout all this growth, development and change, MM Group has remained a family business both in nature and in structure, Vera's grandsons Ian and Michael joined their father in the company in the early 1990s and Trevor Perkins son, Raymond also joined in the 1990s. There is an excellent community spirit among the workforce, and they all share a strong sense of involvement in all the company's undertakings; a lively newsletter, Inside MMG, reports on all happenings - both social and professional - within the Group, keeps employees informed of all developments and invites them to participate in the day-to-day running of the company. One of the most recent schemes to be launched is the Progress Opportunity Programme, POP for short, which offers gift vouchers and substantial cash prizes as incentives for employees to come up with bright ideas to improve working practices.

The company started by artist Vera Hughes truly has evolved into a masterpiece. In less than 50 years MM Group has grown from a small coupon-handling and mail fulfilment operation to a company with an unsurpassed depth and breadth of marketing expertise, helping small clients to grow and clients who are already household names to reach the 24-hour global market which was virtually undreamed-of when the company started; and with technological progress expected to continue apace, MM Group looks forward to an equally exciting future.

Above: *Modern publications for the direct mail industry from Mail Marketing.*

The streets of change

Below: How many motorists left glass from their headlights scattered across the tarmac, or drove home with a dent in their door as a result of this 'meeting of the ways'? The drivers of vehicles travelling from Colston Street to Broad Quay needed to be very aware of traffic from College Green to Colston Avenue, as the two flows of traffic met in the centre (on occasions harder than they had intended!) like the two blades of a pair of scissors. Later traffic schemes and redevelopment thankfully put paid to the age old confusion that had beset motorists for many years.

This pigeon's eye view, possibly shot from an upper window of Colston Hall, takes in the zebra crossings that ensuring the safety of the pedestrian. The crossings linked the wide end of the street by way of a large traffic island which now no longer exists, and here a bus stops to allow people to cross (though not everyone is using the crossing). It is difficult to believe that road safety was an even bigger problem in the early days of motoring than it is today. But between the two world wars a staggering 120,000 people were killed on British roads. The Minister of Transport, Leslie Hore Belisha, decided it was time to do something about it and called for new regulations. He introduced the first pedestrian crossings, and in 1934 the Road Traffic Act brought in the speed limit of 30mph in built up areas and made driving tests compulsory for new drivers.

Some of these lovely buildings have gone, victims of the second world war, and the names above the windows as well as the fashion in shop blinds have changed. This was College Green on a sunny day in March 1938, and a number of people were out enjoying the fresh air and sunshine that heralded the coming of spring. Park Street carries the eye up the hill towards the University Tower, standing guard like a quiet sentinel, honouring the tradition of further education and the name of one of the city's eminent businessmen. On the right, the tower of St Mark's church adds its own touch of character to the scene. The view will immediately put gourmet readers in mind of the nearby Harveys Wine Cellars, where wine has been produced since 1796. The Cellars today attract a large number of visitors who can join a guided tour and see for themselves exactly how their favourite wines are produced, and after enjoying the unique atmosphere of the 13th century wine cellars they can sample the various light or sparkling wines, sherries or port - no doubt the most popular part of the visit! Harveys award-winning restaurant has deservedly found its way into the leading food guides and serves more than 300 wines at widely-ranging prices from its cellars.

Reece Winstone Archive

A mere six years after the end of the second world war, the Festival of Britain kicked off the new decade, infusing Bristol with a spirit of new hope and faith in the future. The years of austerity and deprivation were, it was hoped, in the past. Banners hung around the city and in shop windows, and the Festival's symbol could be seen everywhere, even picked out in colour in our flower beds. The Clifton Suspension Bridge was the icing on Bristol's cake; illuminated from end to end the bridge was an awe-inspiring sight after dark. The Centre Gardens were awash with colour, and this evocative photograph, taken on 24th July 1951, will take readers on a trip down Memory Lane. Temple Meads station was also decked out for the occasion, and a large image of Britannia sat atop a colourful canopy above the station's entrance, transforming Temple Meads into a medieval

A glance at the 1950s

WHAT'S ON?
Television hit Britain in a big way during the 1950s. Older readers will surely remember 'Double Your Money, Dixon of Dock Green and 'Dragnet' (whose characters' names were changed 'to protect the innocent'). Commercial television was introduced on 22nd September 1955, and Gibbs SR toothpaste were drawn out of the hat to become the first advert to be shown. Many believed adverts to be vulgar, however, and audiences were far less than had been hoped for.

GETTING AROUND
The year 1959 saw the development of the world's first practical air-cushion vehicle - better known to us as the hovercraft. The earliest model was only able to travel at slow speeds over very calm water and was unable to carry more than three passengers. The faster and smoother alternative to the sea ferry quickly caught on, and by the 1970s a 170-ton car-carrying hovercraft service had been introduced across the English Channel.

SPORTING CHANCE
The four-minute mile had remained the record since 1945, and had become regarded as virtually unbreakable. On 6th May 1954, however, Oxford University student Roger Bannister literally ran away with the record, accomplishing the seemingly impossible in three minutes 59.4 seconds. Bannister collapsed at the end of his last amazing lap, even temporarily losing his vision. By the end of the day, however, he had recovered suffi-ciently to celebrate his achievement in a London night club!

Camelot. Visitors to the city arriving and departing by train could not fail to be impressed by the scale of the festivities and the welcome they received. Those who could afford to make the trip, of course, went to London, the true centre of festivities. The Festival was held on a reclaimed bomb site, where an incredible £8 million was spent on constructing imaginative buildings to celebrate Britain's industry, architecture, art and design.

Below: Persil was still washing whiter back in 1954, when this photograph of Victoria Street was taken. Adverts showing the contrast between the white shirts or dresses that had been washed in Persil and the greying ones of those that had not were very much a part of Persil's advertising campaign in the 1950s. Rebuilding after the wartime bombing that wiped out so much of the city had yet to begin, and the land to the left of Victoria Street eventually saw the development of modern office blocks to replace these advertisement hoardings. Later years would see the Jaguar car showroom built here, together with the offices of the Transport and General Workers Union. The DRG building was constructed further along the road. Looking towards Bristol Bridge and the city centre from the corner of Mitchell Lane, the Shakespeare pub - still just as alive today as it ever was - can be seen on the right of the photograph, with the Temple Church nearby.
The nostalgia of old adverts is continued near the right edge of the photograph with the well known and rather romantic Players Navy Cut sailor. With 'Invincible' on his cap and a destroyer in the background, he smokes a contented pipe while reading his letter from home.

Right: Even in wartime, road building must go on, especially in such a traffic-congested city as Bristol. The photograph, taken in November 1940, reveals that the work on the road was progressing well; only a few days later, however, the first bombs were to fall on the city and work of a different kind had to begin, with the demolition of bombed buildings, clearance and making the site safe taking priority. Nazi bombing raids could not destroy the life and vigour of The Centre, however, and today this is still seen as the city's centre of culture. Within a short walk of a quarter of a mile or so are the New Vic, Bristol Old Vic, Colston Hall and the wonderful old Hippodrome, still wowing audiences after nearly 90 years. The Hippodrome was built as a 2,000 seat theatre with a gallery, circle and stalls - above which was a dome which opened for ventilation - an ingenious forerunner of air conditioning! Following a highly successful two-week experiment into the 'talkies' - the jungle film 'Congorilla' saw a total sellout of almost every seat - the Hippodrome became a cinema in September 1932. Talkies were a runaway success and were here to stay - though not at the Hippodrome. It was live theatre at heart, and showed its last film in 1938. Its ballets, operas, concerts and musicals have charmed people ever since, and today sees many touring West End shows staged within its historic walls.

Reece Winstone Archive

Reece Winstone Archive

Above: These unusual traffic lights consisting of a red and green only sequence were installed on Bristol Bridge. Similar lights had been set up in other cities around the country, many of them including a notice beneath the traffic lights that instructed motorists to 'move only on green'. This was part of an experiment in omitting the red-amber sequence to try to stop drivers setting off before the lights changed to green; it seems that 'amber gamblers' who race away before the green light appears are not just a product of the 1990s! A police officer on point duty reinforces the rules. A forerunner of the pelican crossings of today, these particular traffic lights also included a side light that told pedestrians when it was safe to cross the road. How strange that the idea was not taken up nationally long before it did catch on; this photograph dates from December 1939. George's Brewery, seen in the background, had celebrated their 150th anniversary the previous year, the dates above the clock proudly announcing the event. George's were Bristol's largest brewer, expanding through a series of take-overs of their rivals. In the mid 1950s the company took over the Bristol United Brewery - their largest competitor. George's were themselves taken over by Courage in 1961.

Right: Looking towards Queen Square in 1948 we see that by this time the much-needed air raid shelters in The Centre have been removed, and for the time being the site is being used as a car park by Bristol motorists, as eager as ever to find a few feet of space in the city where they can leave their cars for a few hours. The view takes in the Arnolfini Arts Centre at the end of the quay, whose buildings form part of Bristol's rich trading history. Based in 160-year-old tea warehouses built for Acraman, Bush, Castle & Co, the gallery leads the way in exhibiting modern art, and has become known for the somewhat 'avant-garde' flavour of some of its productions. The following year was to see many changes to the Bridgehead, when the head of the Frome was landscaped and the cast lead statue of Neptune moved to the position it occupies today. Neptune reminds Bristolians of their seafaring history, and in particular the triangular trade that once took place between Bristol, West Africa and the Caribbean. Britain was by the 18th century one of the leading slave-trading countries. For many years voices of protest were ignored, but the campaign against the slave trade eventually led to its abolition in 1807. It was to be a further 30 years before enslaved people were given their freedom, however.

A typical traffic snarl-up on Bristol Bridge before Redcliffe Way was built to ease the situation. These commuters were most probably trying desperately to get home at the end of a long day, and private cars, push bikes, trams and commercial vehicles creep along nose to tail in this build up of rush hour traffic. This Fry's delivery van, advertising the company's cocoa and chocolate on its rear doors, is likely to have been on its way back to the factory after supplying local shops with a fresh batch of chocolate cream bars, Turkish Delight, Crunchie bars and 'Five Boys' chocolate. Wonderful stuff. When this photograph was taken in 1937 Fry's had only recently lost their gift showroom and offices in Union Street, which were demolished the previous year and were replaced by the Odeon and a number of shops. Traffic problems, it seems, have always been with us in Bristol; even before World War II there were a large number of private cars around the city (though for the majority of ordinary families, owning their own car was an unattainable dream). The problem was not only Bristol's; in fact across the country the number of cars on Britain's roads increased from around 200,000 to more than a million between the end of World War I in 1918 and 1930.

Eeece Winstone Archive

Above: 'Allo, 'allo - wot's goin' on 'ere? A practice run for 'The Bill' perhaps? Or should it be 'Birds of a Feather'? This amusing diversion taking place on Bristol Bridge was nothing more than a swan that had left its usual haunts and decided to take a look around the streets of the city. Pursued along Victoria Street and into Redcliffe Street, the swan with the wanderlust was finally arrested and taken into police custody on Bristol Bridge. With the long arm of the law firmly in control and tucked around its middle, the bird had its rights read before being resolutely carried away to be safely returned to its watery home. After its brush with the law we have to hope that that was the last time it would decide to go swanning around. The incident gave passers by - who had congregated on Fear's Corner to watch the goings on - a lot of amusement, and a bedtime story of a different kind to tell the children that evening.

The scene was captured in April 1939, a matter of months before the outbreak of the second world war. As we know, the Blitz was to change the Bristol landscape for ever, and most of the buildings seen here in Victoria Street were destined to be destroyed in the Nazi bombing raids.

Reece Winstone Archive

Above: Quay Head, 1956, and scaffolding surrounds the new Stonebridge House, built on the site of the pre-war electricity offices. The new electricity showroom faced The Centre, its elegant curves bringing much deserved praise for its imaginative design. By the mid 1950s, post-war prosperity was becoming a reality for many families in the city, and electrical gadgets of every kind were on most 'must have' lists.

Since World War II had liberated them to go out to work, more women than ever were bringing a second income into the home. Their mothers had been content to stay at home and do the washing every Monday with a dolly tub, rubbing board and mangle; they had cooked for the family on a gas ring or an old kitchen range; they had scrubbed floors, and swept and beaten carpets and rugs. But now it was the 1950s, and for the first time women had the extra cash to go out and buy that refrigerator, electric mixer, vacuum cleaner, electric iron and washing machine. It was the decade that made television viewing popular, ushered in the attitude of 'keeping up with the Joneses' and buying goods on the 'never never', paying a few shillings each week on account.

Right: Bristol is virtually unrecognisable as the same city in this aerial view captured on camera in the late 1930s. Row after row of shops, houses, businesses and services from the left bank towards the top of the picture were destined to disappear from the city map, and today the green space of Castle Park with its pleasant waterside walk offers Bristolians and visitors alike a breath of fresh air. At the top of the photograph the chimneys of Fry's chocolate factory can be seen, well remembered by those who worked there as well as those who enjoyed the end product!

Near Bristol Bridge readers will recognise the spire of St Nicholas's church, with St Nicholas's market opposite. The church was one of the many places of worship that were blitzed during World War II, but St Nicholas's was to be given a new lease of life, and lived on as the Bristol Tourist Information Centre. The area today is largely commercial, having a large number of solicitors and accountants. The other side of Bristol Bridge also saw much redevelopment, with new office blocks including the Dickinson Robinson Group replacing many of the old waterside properties. Further along, the Courage Brewery still dispenses liquid refreshment; how many readers remember their first pint of Home Brew Split?

Above: Spot anything familiar about this scene? Bristolians who have had to cope with the more recent disruptions of the late 1990s, when contractors and their machinery arrived to dig up the centre gardens in order to provide the city with a pleasant pedestrian area will immediately identify. This image was captured some 60 years ago, when the gardens were still under construction, and the barrage balloons that fly high above the city tell us that it was wartime. 'No hat, no boots, no job' is the principle followed by today's workers, however, and areas that might prove dangerous to the public are always carefully fenced off. The shops, the businesses and the adverts will be well remembered by mature readers who patronised Willways Garage and whiled away an hour over a pot of tea at Paynes cafe (who also offered Bed and Breakfast). They may even remember the huge marmalade advert that told them rather cleverly 'Golden Shred puts the taste on the toast', and the rather sweet golly that pleased many a child in those far off days when political correctness was not an issue. The Sedan Chair survives and is still a popular watering hole, offering thirsty Bristolians a pint or two of their favourite brew. We all know the slogan 'Bovril prevents that sinking feeling'; written before World War I, the saying was withheld to respect those lost on the 'Titanic' in 1912.

Right: Bedminster Bridge was constructed in 1882, and over the years it was to grow very busy and congested, carrying much of the heavy traffic that travelled between Bristol and Weston Super Mare. The city's answer to the problem was an ingenious one; build a second bridge to the left of Bedminster Bridge and create a one-way system. York Road goes off towards the left and Coronation Road to the right, while Bedminster Parade is straight on. These homes and shops between York Road and Bedminster Parade were demolished in the autumn of 1961 in the road widening scheme, little more than a year after this photograph was taken.

This was a working class area where industry, the docks and the railway all played their part in creating a tight-knit, lively community where people shopped, worked and lived their lives. History of one kind and another was made not too far away, with the Imperial Tobacco factory offering employment to the residents and St Mary Redcliffe Church caring for their spiritual needs. St Mary Redcliff is still one of the city's most well-known churches, offering lunchtime recitals and many other musical events. The church's Undercroft Cafe has proved a popular venue for parties and receptions as well as for the odd cup of coffee and light lunch.

A heartbreaking scene of utter devastation that was echoed around the city of Bristol at the end of the second world war. So many well-known buildings disappeared from this area, among them the Regent Cinema, opened in style in 1928, and St Peter's church. The bombs that obliterated the fine buildings nearer the water's edge missed Fry's chimney, which was to survive as a landmark in the city until 1961. When it was decided to demolish the huge chimney, the top 220 ft was painstakingly removed by steeplejacks, working with hammers and crowbars at dizzying heights far above the ground. The remaining 80 ft was then blown up. If the old and familiar buildings had to go, then a pleasant parkland with a landscaped waterside walk made the best kind of replacement - and younger readers will only know this area as Castle Park.

The shopping habits of the nation have been revolutionised over the years, and the advent of large supermarkets has not all been good news, especially for the small retailer. Undercover shopping, however, became a popular feature of the late 20th century - especially appreciated in the chill winds and driving rain of a British winter. The Galleries Shopping Centre, with more than 100 shops under the same roof, has changed the foreground of this photograph for ever.

On the move

Above: Remember the Ovaltineys? The popular children's club was given advertising space on the side of at least one of the city's trams (long found to be useful as mobile advertisement hoardings!) back in 1939, by which time the club had five million active members. Launched over Radio Luxembourg, the Ovaltineys were given secret codes, comics, badges - and a little book of rules which they were expected to follow. It was the stirring little jingle, though, that really caught on, and even non-members could be heard singing 'We are the Ovaltineys, happy girls and boys....' Readers, we are sure, could sing it right now if hard pressed....
When other cities around the country were getting rid of their quaint old trams with outside stairs and upper decks that were open to the British weather and replacing them with a more up-to-date version, Bristol hung on to theirs until a Luftwaffe bomb put paid to most of the tram routes that still remained. Motor buses, which had replaced horse-drawn omnibuses as early as 1906, took over all the routes in the city - but the nostalgia of the old trams stayed with Bristolians for as long as they could remember them. That will surely include a number of our more mature readers!

Top: It was 4th September 1939, and the war with Germany was a mere 24 hours old. Optimists had long believed that the war would not happen at all, while many others thought that if it did it would all be over very quickly. Those in the know realised that it was better to be on the safe side, however, and in spite of Chamberlain's attempts to appease Adolph Hitler, they began to prepare the citizens of Britain for a conflict they believed was inevitable. Preparations included introducing a ban on street lighting, and white stripes were painted down the centre of roads, on lamp posts, steps and kerbs to help drivers and pedestrians avoid accidents in the blackout. It undoubtedly helped, though the scheme was not 100 percent effective, and inevitably the blackout accounted for a number of accidents - and not only on the roads. An amazing total of 28 people fell into the water, and new signs, 'Danger, open waterfront' were erected. This view along Bedminster Bridge shows that trams 125 and 214 have blank destination blinds - another wartime strategy to ensure that spies would find it difficult to find their way around the city. A great idea as far as local people who knew their route numbers were concerned, but a tad more difficult for strangers to Bristol! Place names and other identifying marks on buildings were also obscured to confuse the enemy about exactly where they were.

A glance at the 1950s

MELODY MAKERS

Few teenage girls could resist the blatant sex-appeal of 'Elvis the Pelvis', though their parents were scandalised at the moody Presley's provocatively gyrating hips. The singer took America and Britain by storm with such hits as 'Jailhouse Rock', 'All Shook Up' and 'Blue Suede Shoes'. The rhythms of Bill Haley and his Comets, Buddy Holly, Chuck Berry, and Roy Orbison (who had a phenomenal three-octave voice) turned the 1950s into the Rock 'n' Roll years.

INVENTION AND TECHNOLOGY

Until the late 1950s you did not carry radios around with you. Radios were listened to at home, plugged into a mains socket in every average sitting room. Japan was in the forefront of electronic developments even then, and in 1957 the Japanese company Sony introduced the world's very first all-transistor radio - an item of new technology that was small enough to fit into your pocket. The major consumer product caught on fast - particularly with teenage listeners.

SCIENCE AND DISCOVERY

DNA (deoxyribonucleic acid) was first defined as long ago as 1953, and the effects have been far-reaching. The key discovery was developed over the following years and today DNA finger-printing has become an accepted part of life. Genetic diseases such as hemophilia and cystic fibrosis have been identified. Criminals are continually detected and brought to justice. Biological drugs have been developed. More controversially, drought and disease-resistant plants have been engineered - and more controversially Dolly the sheep has been produced.

Reece Winstone Archive

A historic image of the opening of a stretch of the M5 Motorway, and a procession of vehicles headed up by the Lord Mayor's Daimler AE 1 are the first vehicles to ceremonially drive along the new highway, officially opening this stretch that was to make so much difference to the city of Bristol and the surrounding areas.

In Bristol, traffic congestion became a problem as far back as the 1930s, when motorists could not find a space to park in the city streets. Various solutions were sought, including new road layouts, one-way traffic systems, and eventually new car parks, parking meters and traffic wardens.

Once the second world war was over and the country began to return to full production, ordinary people found themselves financially able to take on the responsibility of a car, and for the first time began to think about taking a course or two of driving lessons. By the early 1960s one in seven people owned a car, and accidents, pollution and noise prompted drastic plans to help traffic to move faster and avoid town centre bottlenecks. Motorways were introduced in response to the growing traffic problems, speeding the delivery of goods from city to city, and stretch by stretch new motorways were laid down, criss-crossing the country in a network of communication.

'FULL' shouts the sign on the board. But who cares how many people board the last tram? Certainly these passengers, thought to be bound for Brislington, were not worried about breaking the rules for once. As early as 1938 Bristol's trams began to be phased out and replaced by motor buses, and route by route the old-fashioned vehicles were withdrawn and sent to that great tram shed in the sky. Each route had its 'last tram' - and its souvenir hunters, who took away with them everything they could lay their hands on, even if it was nailed down!

How many of the crews' uniform jackets, destination blinds, lamps, handrails and honesty boxes removed from the 'last trams' are still tucked away, half forgotten, in boxes in lofts around Bristol? All those guilty, wave your tram drivers' caps....

It had been planned that every tram should go by the end of the decade, but as events turned out, World War II intervened. Petrol rationing meant that even car owners were using public transport, yet buses were in need of urgent maintenance. Spare parts were like gold dust and were just as elusive, so the trams lived on - until in 1941 a Luftwaffe bomb hit a bridge, severing the trams' power cables and leaving only two workable routes. The end had come at last for Bristol's trams.

Below: Everyone loves a holiday by the sea, and the delights of Torquay and Paignton topped the popularity charts with local people. A wide-brimmed hat for the sun, a coat in case of chilly winds, and a pair of light shoes was what you obviously needed; the rest of your holiday clothes were packed away in your suitcase, which was securely fixed to the luggage rack on top of the coach. Many holidaymakers were treated as friends by the seaside landladies who saw the same families during the same weeks year after year. Once they had checked into their 'digs' there was plenty to do, but first of all the beach beckoned, and children with buckets and spades made a beeline along the promenade and on to the sand to build castles and dig moats that would fill with water as the tide came in. Parents would lounge in a deck chair nearby where they could keep at least one eye on what the children were up to. Rainy days presented no problem to the holidaymakers; amusement arcades, funfairs, shops and the local pubs all presented a welcome change from the realities of working life.

There were many families, of course, who could not afford to get away for a fortnight's holiday, and they eagerly looked forward to the occasional day trip to Ilfracombe, Minehead, Weston-Super-Mare - or even a day out at their own Clifton Zoo.

Right: Shake and rattle if not roll was all part of daily life in the days when the family car was a distant and unattainable dream for most people. Back in the 1930s, if you wanted to go anywhere, whether it was to the cinema, a dance hall or simply to work, you went by public transport - and for many that meant the uncomfortable and draughty though well-loved tram. Only a couple of these passengers appear to be aware of the camera, though had they known about it most of them would have been thrilled to 'have their picture taken'. Though photography was very well-established by the 1930s, few ordinary people had a camera of their own, and the presence of a photographer still held lots of novelty value.

When this image was captured for posterity on 20th August 1938, the days of Bristol's ageing trams were very definitely numbered and had limited time left to them. Replacement of trams with motor buses had begun earlier in the year, and by May 34 trams had already been taken out of service and were on their way to the graveyard; four weeks later the wooden bodies of the historic old vehicles had been burnt and the chassis and wheels taken over by the scrap merchant.

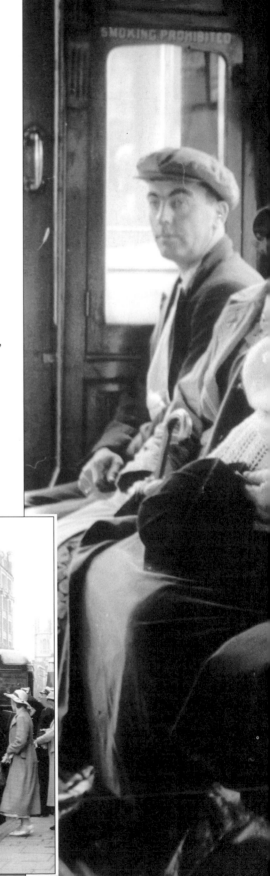

Reece Winstone Archive

Looking in the direction of Lewins Mead, this view of Colston Avenue, taken on 24th January 1956, gives us the unfamiliar sight of traffic running in a counter clockwise direction around the Cenotaph, built in memory of the many in Bristol who gave their lives in the two world wars. The statue of Edward Colston, who died in 1721, was later moved back a little as part of the city's new traffic schemes.

Bristol's rich history, that goes back an incredible one thousand years, is well represented in and around Colston Avenue. Off to the right we would see the tall tower of St Stephen's church - Bristol City Parish Church - where regular concerts and lunchtime recitals are currently held, while off to the left stands the church of St Mary on the Quay. Opened in 1840 by followers of evangelist Edward Irving, the chapel subsequently became a Roman Catholic

A glance at the 1960s

WHAT'S ON?
Television comedy came into its own in the 1960s, and many of the shows that were favourites then went on to become classics. 'On the Buses', 'Steptoe and Son', 'Till Death Us Do Part' and 'The Army Game' kept audiences laughing, while the incredible talents of Morecambe and Wise, the wit of Des O'Connor - often the butt of the duo's jokes - and the antics of Benny Hill established them for ever in the nation's affections.

GETTING AROUND
The 2nd March 1969 was a landmark in the history of aviation. The Anglo-French supersonic airliner Concorde took off for the first time from Toulouse in France. Concorde, which can cruise at almost twice the speed of sound, was designed to fly from London to New York in an incredible three hours twenty minutes. The event took place just weeks after the Boeing 747, which can carry 500 passengers to Concorde's modest 100, made its first flight.

SPORTING CHANCE
Wembley Stadium saw scenes of jubilation when on 30th July 1966 England beat West Germany 4-2 in the World Cup. The match, played in a mixture of sunshine and showers, had been a nailbiting experience for players and spectators alike from the very beginning when Germany scored only thirteen minutes into the game. It was Geoff Hurst's two dramatic goals scored in extra time that secured the victory and lifted the cup for England - at last.

church. Further along is Zed Alley; what a pity nobody seems to know how it got its extraordinary name!
A few minutes' walk would take us on towards Lewins Mead and the impressive Unitarian Chapel that dates from 1791. The chapel replaced an even earlier building, constructed in 1694. Nearby the River Frome still flows, though today it is unseen, having been covered over in the late 1930s.

Shopping spree

Below: A busy morning scene in Baldwin Street as market traders unload their crates of cauliflowers, cabbages, bananas, apples, and all the other items of greengrocery needed to feed the hungry shoppers of Bristol. Other shops nearby included fresh fish - and who remembers the ice shop that stood on the right? In earlier years the ice shop was no doubt successful as few businesses, shops or families owned freezers and refrigerators at that time, and the ready availability of commercially-frozen ice must have been a real boon to them. Such a business was destined for eventual failure, however, as post-war prosperity had put refrigerators within the reach of most families between the mid 1950s and early 60s; this photograph dates from April 1960. The home freezing of garden and allotment produce, baked goods and plated meals enjoyed a lot of popularity in the 1970s. A few decades on, many working couples have little time to cook and freeze food, and for many the freezer has become little more than a storage space for quick and convenient meals.

The scene was to undergo dramatic changes within a few years of this photograph; in 1968 a new fruit and vegetable market was built in St Philips Marsh, and the part of the city around Baldwin Street has become largely a business area, with a number of solicitors and accountants based here.

The people of Bristol love a good celebration, and the Coronation of King George VI back in 1937 gave them an ideal excuse to really go to town. The ceremony on 12th May was broadcast to the nation; many families still did not have a wireless set of their own - but a large number of those who did have one gathered on College Green to hear the radio broadcast from High Cross. The event became a wonderful social occasion to be remembered and talked about for years afterwards. Albert, Duke of York, had been hurled unexpectedly into the kingship he had not been trained for when his older brother Edward VIII, who had been king for a mere 325 days, renounced the throne on 10th December 1936. The new King was shy and nervous and suffered from an embarrassing stammer (which he later overcame with medical aid and the support of his wife Queen Elizabeth). 'I'm only a naval officer,' he confessed to his cousin Lord Louis Mountbatten on the day he became King. 'It's the only thing I know about.' He had never seen a state paper in his life. But he rose to the challenge, squared his shoulders, and adopted the title of George VI. King George went on to take his place as perhaps Britain's most well loved monarch.

A glance at the 1960s

HOT OFF THE PRESS

Barbed wire, concrete blocks and a wide no-man's-land divided East from West when a reinforced wall was built right across the city of Berlin in 1961. Many East Germans escaped to the West at the eleventh hour, taking with them only the possessions they could carry. The Berlin Wall divided the city - and hundreds of family members and friends - for 28 years until the collapse of Communist rule across Eastern Europe. Who can ever forget those scenes in 1989, when ordinary people themselves began to physically tear down the hated wall?

THE WORLD AT LARGE

'One giant leap for mankind' was taken on 20th July 1969, when Neil Armstrong made history as the first man to set foot on the Moon. During the mission he and fellow-astronaut 'Buzz' Aldrin collected rock and soil samples, conducted scientific experiments - and had a lot of fun jumping around in the one-sixth gravity. Twenty-one hours and thirty-seven minutes after their landing they took off again in their lunar module 'Eagle' to rejoin Apollo II which was orbiting above them, proudly leaving the American flag on the Moon's surface.

ROYAL WATCH

Princess Margaret's announcement in 1960 that she was to wed photographer Antony Armstrong-Jones (later Lord Snowdon) brought sighs of relief from her immediate family. Just five years earlier the people of Britain had sympathised as the princess bowed to public and private pressure, ending her relationship with Peter Townsend, Prince Philip's former equerry. The Church (and the Queen, as its Head) frowned on the liaison as Townsend was divorced. Her marriage to Lord Snowdon itself ended in 1978.

The huge crown in the Centre Gardens reminds us that this photograph, taken from the corner of Clare Street, dates from coronation year, 1953, and a second glance reveals the flags and bunting flutter from every available pole and flagstaff. Do you remember the Hippodrome when it still had its tower and globe? This is the way the historic theatre looked before both were removed in 1964. The theatre-goers of Bristol were in for a treat on that particular week in June, as

Julie Andrews, the 'Sound of Music' star with the golden voice, was billed along with the comedian Max Wall. Colston Hall, just off the right of the photograph, was rebuilt in 1951 to celebrate the Festival of Britain; fire swept through the building in February 1945 - the second time the hall had been destroyed by fire. Many readers will recognise the clock that gave us 'Guinness Time'. Guinness has been sold in Bristol for more than 100 years, and it was here that the first Guinness Store in Great Britain was opened in 1875. The British public have believed that the drink was good for them since it was first advertised in 1929. Many clever slogans have been produced over the years: 'Tall, Dark and Have Some', 'Seven Million Every Day and Still Going Down', and notably 'I've Never Tried it Because I Don't Like it'. And remember 'Guinness is Good for you - Just think what Toucan do'?

How long did these ladies have to wait for their dates to arrive? Our sympathies are with them as they wait patiently on the corner of Old Market Street, their eyes scanning Carey's Lane for two hurrying males (could the girls hope they'd be carrying chocolates to make up for keeping them waiting?). We have no record of their names, but these girls formed an unwitting part in a little piece of the city's history, as the place where they waited for their elusive dates back in 1961 now no longer exists. The Kings Cinema was to close in 1976 after a long and eventful history which started back in 1910, when its predecessor opened as the Kings Hall. Its elegant entrance hall and staircases, decorated in gold and white, added an air of luxury to the awe-inspiring magic of those wonderful early films. The cinema went through extensive extensions in 1920, reopening a year later with 1,485 seats. A fire in 1926 let to further restoration. When the Kings opened its doors once again the costs for the cheapest seats had risen by a penny, but the more affluent cinemagoers could still get in for a shilling. The great attraction was that most of the films shown there were accompanied by the 12-piece Kings Symphony Orchestra. The Kings Cinema boomed through the 'talkies', winged its way through wartime, and survived Cinemascope - only to be in the end defeated by television.

At work

Debate, discussion, disagreement and plain old opposition marked the building of the Council House. Architect E Vincent Harris's design was approved in 1934 (though the committee had been considering the scheme since 1919), and the following year the work at last got underway, starting with the demolition of old properties on College Green. Sensitively faced with light brown hand-made bricks that would not detract from the nearby cathedral, the new building swept around College Green in a long, elegant Georgian-style crescent; so far so good. Bristolians, however, were not at all taken with the rest of the design, which involved lowering College Green to street level so that the new municipal building could be seen more clearly, and

removing the High Cross - a replica of the medieval cross that once stood there (today at Stourhead House, Warminster). Replica or not, Bristol did not see why they should part with their historic landmark, and they went to war with the planners. Their fight to save it was only partly successful, but the upper part of the cross was saved and now stands in Berkeley Square in Clifton. Queen Victoria's statue had also been removed but the great monarch was later returned after a public campaign.

The ornamental moat, too, came in for some criticism after an unwary motorist drove his car into it. Once the ripples had calmed, however, the Council House 'settled in' and over the years became an accepted part of the Bristol landscape.

COWLIN

As early as the 1930s motorists were finding it increasingly difficult to find a parking place in Bristol city centre, and in 1936 a leaflet was issued by the Council - 'Where to Park Your Car in the Centre of Bristol'. The problem of congestion in the city remained and work began the same year on an inner ring road which would link major roads and hopefully keep the heaviest traffic away from the city streets. The new Temple Way was laid down and a new route cut through the city, its course involving the demolition of various properties including the Merchants Arms pub, and the covering in of part of the River Frome. Bristol's traffic problem remained,

however - mainly because more people were buying a family car; the number of car owners actually doubled between 1950 and 1961!

Bomb sites were the obvious choice for car parking, and in 1960 Bristol's very first multi-storey car park was built in Rupert Street, partly using the site of an old Victorian brewery that had been destroyed in the second world war. Attempts to regulate parking around the city continued, with parking meters being introduced in 1961 (Bristol was the first city outside London to install them) - along with 25 traffic wardens who patrolled the streets to make sure that people used them.

The family firm at home on Union Street for 110 years

In 1889 Charles Kemp, who had been working in his elder brother's jewellery shop in the then fashionable shopping area of Stokes Croft, went into business with his younger brother Edward, who was working at the Goldsmiths' Alliance on College Green. Their father William, an accountant, lent them £400, a considerable sum in those days when clerks were beginning to aspire to the level of £1 a week in remuneration, with which to start a business of their own. A fourth Kemp brother was able to supply them with stock from his wholesale clock business in Bridge Street. Businesses, like clocks, run on wheels within wheels.

Above: Charles Wilson Kemp with his wife Ella.
Right: The macabre Skull and Crossbones tobacco box, manufactured for the Bristol Savages in 1914.
Below: Kemp Brother's shop in 1931, at number 4 Union Street.

The two new merchant adventurers opened their Watchmakers and Jewellers shop at No. 4 Union Street, ideally located on the edge of the major shopping quarter bounded by Wine Street and Castle Street. Today No. 4, at the top of Union Street, is near the entrance to the Galleries Shopping Centre. Following the age-old custom of their trade they not only sold but bought old gold, silver and gems, whose value rarely drops.

Edward Kemp left Bristol for Leicester in 1900 leaving Charles to carry on aided by H E Tyrell, who stayed for forty years and became a partner soon after Edward's departure. Twelve years later the firm was strengthened by the addition of Charles' son Milford and, a year later, by Sidney and, in 1921 by his third son Clifford. Milford's two sons, Brian and Michael, also came into the business and most recently Brian's daughter Margaret has become the fourth generation of the family in the

firm after abandoning her career as a Ward Sister at Southmead Hospital.

Soon after the founding of the business Kemp Brothers began making turret clocks, these were designed and made on the premises, patterns being made in wood and then cast by a firm in Fishponds. On 15th November 1899 Queen Victoria opened the Convalescent Home, (near the Downs) later to become Bristol Maternity Hospital and now used as offices. As she sat outside in her carriage she pressed a button to open the Home and also to start the clock that had been made by Kemp Brothers. But the pressing of the button only rang a bell in the clock tower and it was one of the Kemp Brothers' clock-makers who actually set the clock going.

Another clock made by Kemp Brothers is in the Urijah Thomas Memorial at the top of Blackboy Hill. The original dial and hands of this memorial clock are still in place but the first mechanical movement has been replaced with an electric one. Other well known clocks made by the firm included the chime clock on the former Pro-Cathedral, continuing the early Kemp tradition of making, installing and servicing church tower clocks. The old Western Daily Press premises in Baldwin Street bore a Kemp Brothers clock dating from the days when few carried watches and relied on visible clocks on public buildings for their time keeping. Charles Hill's Dockyard was another such clock upon which a once vital area of the Bristol economy relied. Some of the firm's clocks were also sent abroad, one was installed at Peking Railway Station in the early 1900s when the British and French ran the Chinese power and communications systems.

As well as clocks the manufacture of silver and silver-plated goods was also carried out on the premises. Charles Kemp had been unable to buy articles that he thought were of a high enough standard to sell in his shop and so decided to make them himself. Tea sets, cake baskets, tankards, spoons and forks among other things were made in solid silver and silver plate. There was a polishing shop with four electric motors and the largest silver plating vat in the West of England. The workshops were always busy, but during the First World War they had to be closed half an hour early because of the restriction on the use of electricity. When Milford Kemp came into the business he combined his duties in the shop with travelling the South West of England selling the 'Kembro' plate to hotels, restaurants and the then popular ice-cream parlours.

Special commissions were also made by the skilled craftsmen in the silver-smith workshop, including a model of a Racing Skiff in 9ct gold. The seats and foot rockers moved as in a real Skiff, and it was so much admired that two more were made in solid silver. The Skull and Crossbones Tobacco Box in silver (pictured) was made in 1914 for the Bristol Savages and is still in evidence at each of their meetings. By 1933 the firm was expanding and took over, Fisher and Co's shop next door and towards the end of the 1930s was employing fifty people.

Above: An Indenture for an apprentice named John Jones dated 1899. He went on to work for the firm as clockmaker for forty years until he was tragically killed on December 8th 1942 in a road accident, in the blackout, returning to work after winding clocks. Below: The devastation caused during the Blitz in 1940.

award to jewellers taking the rigorous world-wide examination to gain their Fellowship Diploma. At present the firm has a number of staff who have also taken various examinations set by allied professional bodies and the present clockmaker served his five-year apprenticeship with the firm.

The staff at Kemp Brothers have always been very loyal and many spent a good part of their working lives with the firm. A silversmith who worked for the firm for 58 years holds the record and the majority of present employees have been with the firm for over ten years.

Satisfied customers who buy their first pieces, be it a good watch or an engagement ring from a jewellers providing the standard of service that they get at Kemp Brothers, return time and time again to mark milestones in their lives with gifts and mementoes as their fortunes and families swell. Such investments can be sold and upgraded to more up-to-date designs whenever required.

The firm became a Limited Company in 1978 but is still a family owned business with three family members taking an active role in the day-to-day operations. They pride themselves on offering a personal service, quality and value with a wide range of stock including nine and 18ct gold jewellery and gem jewellery, exclusive watches, silverware and giftware.

Unfortunately the building of which 29 Union Street forms a part is to be redeveloped and for the second time in 110 years the company is forced to move home. Fortunately they are only moving two doors down the road making Kemp Brothers the only shop in Broadmead to have successfully traded in the same street for more than a century.

Above left: The shop at 29 Union Street as it appeared shortly after the war. *Below:* The new shop, which opened on the 9th April 1999, taking Kemp Brothers into the new Millennium.

All this came to a disastrous end when the Blitz of 24th November 1940 totally destroyed much of the Bristol shopping centre including Kemp Brother's shop and factory, the building burning for several days as several tons of coal had just been delivered for the boiler fire. Fortunately a shop near to the Odeon Cinema at 29 Union Street was vacant. Four months later Kemp Brothers moved into their new premises after conducting business from temporary quarters in the former J S Fry & Sons, the Quaker chocolate makers, offices in Broadmead. The manufacturing side of the business ceased and all but three of the skilled workers were assigned to war work.

Luxury items such as jewellery were simultaneously in demand and in short supply during the war making it difficult to maintain stocks. The second hand section of their trade rose to supply the deficit and the variable purchase tax payable at the time of purchase by the retailer on many classes of goods rose at one time to 125%.

Kemp Brothers have always tried to maintain a high standard of trained staff and in 1953 Brian Kemp sat the examination set by the Gemmological Association, the jewellers' professional body, and was awarded the Tully Medal. This is the Gemmalogical Association's highest

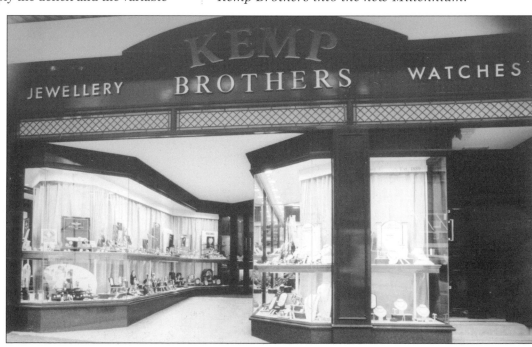

Bristol's 'safe haven'

Throughout history, people's prime concerns have been health, wealth and happiness. Unfortunately nobody can guarantee happiness - though a number of recipes, from the religious to the sacrilegious, have been tried. Reasonable steps can be taken to safeguard wealth through sensible investment and financial planning. Health is perhaps the most important of the three, and whilst it is not possible to eliminate the risk of disease or illness, we can at least protect ourselves from its consequences by joining one of the excellent healthcare schemes which have been in existence for many years; and of these schemes none is longer-established or better designed than those of the Bristol Contributory Welfare Association Limited.

It seems that high cost of providing medical care has always been a problem. During the early 1920s, the Voluntary Hospitals which were the only source of treatment for many people were facing a financial crisis. In 1926 representatives of the Bristol Royal Infirmary, Bristol General Hospital and various works committees met and, no

Above: Alderman E. Brookhouse-Richards JP, the first President of the Bristol Medical Institutions Contributory Scheme.
Right: An ambulance used to transport the Scheme members around in 1940.

doubt mindful of the recommendations made by the Government Committee which had looked into this particular problem some little while earlier, agreed upon a scheme which would 'raise funds for the upkeep of all institutions on the list and on behalf of these entitled to benefit, making provision for the whole or part payment of the charges for maintenance of the same.' Funds would be raised by regular contributions from working people and citizens generally and used to provide an assured income for the hospitals, while contributors and their families would not be charged for any hospital treatment which they might need. Contributions were set at twopence a week and special provision was made for those with an annual income of more than £312, who were not entitled to treatment in the public wards of voluntary hospitals.

Thus the Bristol Medical Institutions Contributory Scheme began, with Mr James Tudor as Honorary Secretary. During its first year 102 companies and other organisations in Bristol made arrangements for their employees to join the scheme if they wished, and income totalled £1,333. Regular contributors and members of their family who needed hospital treatment would receive a voucher, which was known as a 'blue card', to be handed over to the hospital almoner, and at the end of each month each hospital would submit an account to BMICS detailing the number of in-patients and out-patients treated, and BMICS would make the appropriate payment.

Over the next few years the prime concern of the scheme seems to have shifted slightly from the upkeep of the hospitals to the needs of the contributors. On 20th February 1935, working on the basis of its experience in administering the scheme, the Committee agreed a proposal whereby contributors could choose to pay an extra penny a week which

would entitle them to a cash payment of one guinea (£1-1s-0d, or £1.05p) per week during a hospital stay of up to six weeks. This was to compensate for loss of earnings when the breadwinner was in hospital, and the payment was also made when it was the wife who was admitted to hospital as this would have incurred additional domestic expenses. Although the new Extended Benefits Scheme displeased the Joint Committee of Hospital Representatives who saw it as 'inimical to the interests of the Voluntary Hospitals', it proved popular with contributors, and in April 1935 the adminis-tration of the two complementary sections of the fund was split, with the Bristol Contributory Scheme Welfare Association being set up to administer the extended scheme under the auspices of the BMICS. The new Association was headed by James Tudor. A central location for the headquarters was sought for the convenience of members, and offices were set up at Welfare House, 95 Stapleton Road.

Bristol Contributory Scheme Welfare Association.

Established 1935.

This Booklet contains particulars of

... A PLAN ...

whereby YOU may safeguard yourself (or dependents) against the risk of heavy expenditure arising from

SURGICAL OPERATIONS,

SPECIALIST CONSULTATIONS

and **BED COSTS** in Nursing Homes or Hospitals.

No INCOME LIMITS for Membership

Around the time that the Extended scheme was introduced, seven hospitals were listed as providing free treatment under the BMICS scheme: Bristol Royal Infirmary, Bristol General Hospital, Women and Children's Hospital, Bristol Homoeopathic Hospital, Bristol Eye Hospital, Orchard St Eye Dispensary, and Cossham Memorial Hospital; and the BMICS prospectus neatly defined the scheme's twofold reasons for existence as: ' The hospitals need a large and more assured income; the wage earner may need the hospital one day and does not want to make heavy payments at hospital at a time when he can least afford it'.

BCSWA instituted separate arrangements, which formed Section II of the scheme, to cater for hose earning in excess of £312. Section II was more complex and was run by its own Executive Committee, who refined and modified the scheme over the years, as circumstances dictated. Contributions could be made at either Scale A rate or the Scale B rate, which gave higher benefits. The trend seems to have been for benefits to increase

while contribution rates remained fixed. In 1942, for instance, the contribution rate remained at one guinea a year on Scale A and one and a half guineas on Scale B, but the benefits were extended to provide an additional one guinea per week towards bed costs, raising the weekly payment from four guineas to five guineas on Scale A and five to six guineas on Scale B. An 'extra cover' option was also introduced, whereby an extra five shillings a year brought an additional five guineas towards surgeons' fees. Without this 'extra cover' the contribution towards surgeons' fees was ten guineas on Scale A and 15 guineas on Scale B. Assistance with consultants' fees on Scale A stood at £2-2s-0d for consultations at the patient's own residence and £1-1s-0d if the patient visited a consulting room. By 1947 a contribution of one guinea (one and a half guineas on Scale B) towards Operating Theatre Fees had been added, and the contribution towards surgeons' costs, without taking out the 'extra cover' option, had been increased to twelve guineas (20 guineas on Scale B). However, by this time the National Health Act had been passed, which when it was imple-mented on 5th July 1948 would hand over responsibility for funding and running the hospitals to the State, and this brought into question the whole future of contributory schemes.

The British Hospitals Contributory Schemes Association set up a Committee to investigate whether there was a role for contrib-utory schemes under the new health service provision. Whereas many towns and cities had run schemes similar to that

Above: *A leaflet from the 1930s outlining the benefits of the Scheme.*
Right: *Mr J S Tudor, appointed first Honorary Secretary in 1926.*

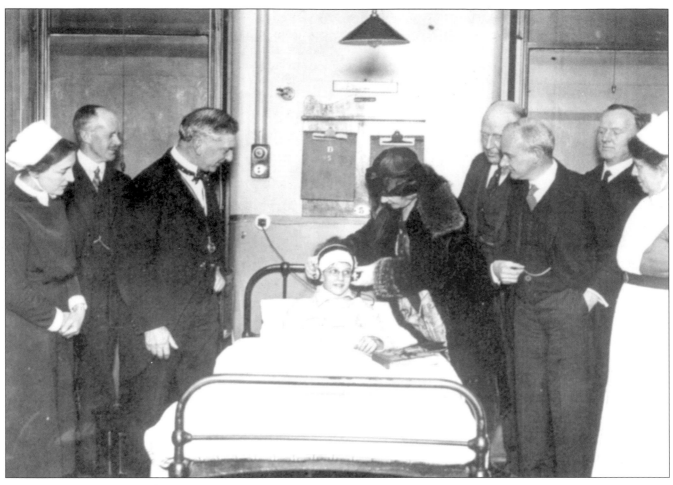

begun by BMICS, Bristol's scheme was the only one which had developed into the provision of welfare benefits and provision for private patients, and BMICS's experience was therefore invaluable in showing that peace of mind and freedom from financial anxiety was an aid to the recovery of hospital patients. The eventual decision was that whilst Contributory Schemes were no longer required to fund the Voluntary Hospitals, they had a valuable role to play provided they followed the lead given by BCWA. Some of the small local schemes closed down, some merged to form larger schemes, and some, like BCWA, elected to remain independent.

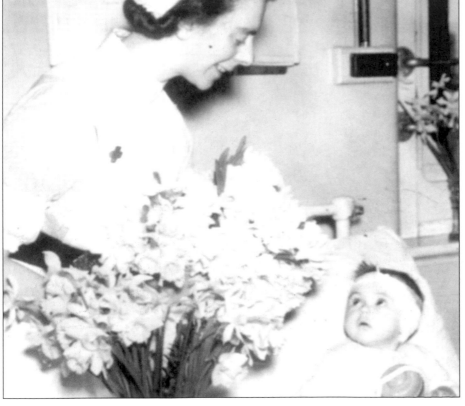

It was thought that the introduction of the National Health Service would reduce the incentive of joining private health plans; however, BCWA's membership from 1948 continued to grow, partly no doubt due to the long waiting lists for admission to general wards, and partly due to BCWA's success in offering a good deal to its members. In 1948 its Hospital Scheme offered the highest benefit rate in the country for the lowest contribution rate - £2-9s-0d per week for a contribution of 2d a week - but by 1951 expenditure on benefits was considerably

Top: *A typical ward in a voluntary hospital.* ***Left:*** *One of BCWA's children's wards in the late 1950s.*

exceeding its income from contributions, so the rates had to be revised to restore viability.

In 1953 it was necessary to extend the Association's offices, and the resulting building, at 95-97 Stapleton Road, was renamed Tudor House in memory of James Tudor. The Honorary Secretary of the Association at this time was Geoffrey Wren, who was succeeded on his retirement in 1976 by his son Martin, the grandson of James Tudor. The Association remained at Tudor House until 1967, when it moved to Victoria Street; it moved into Bristol House in Victoria Street in 1978, and finally to its present home at James Tudor House, still in Victoria Street, in December 1996.

Throughout the remainder of the 50s, the 60s and the early 70s both the Hospital Scheme and the Private Patients Scheme continued to thrive. Many employers, including Bristol Corporation, entered into an agreement with BCWA to deduct employee's contributions at source, and as BCWA's good

reputation began to spread its members were drawn from an increasingly wide geographical area. The benefits to NHS patients were soon extended to cover such items such as dentures, spectacles, physiotherapy treatment and convalescence costs, and as NHS charges increased, first a two-tier system and then a wider range of payment options were introduced to give members the choice of either continuing to contribute at a nominal level, or paying in more and receiving higher benefits. Meanwhile the growth in private patient membership repeatedly made it possible to increase benefits while maintaining contributions at their existing levels. The range of contributory scales meant that the scheme was flexible enough to suit people in all income bands, and in April 1973 the 'Extra Security Scale' was introduced for private patients who wanted complete peace of

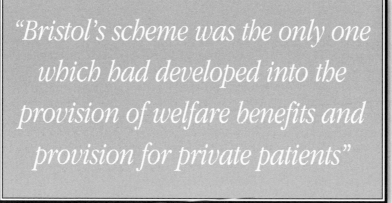

"Bristol's scheme was the only one which had developed into the provision of welfare benefits and provision for private patients"

Below: *Tudor House, 95/97 Stapleton Road, following refurbishment in 1953 and renamed in memory of the late J S Tudor, founder, Secretary and Chairman of the Association.*

mind; this scale simply provided full reimbursements of all in-patient costs.

During the mid 1970s the government began to phase out the provision for private beds in NHS hospitals, and in 1975 pay-bed charges were increased by 50 percent at a stroke, which forced BCWA to review its liabilities and the position of its members. Contributions to the Extra Security Scale were increased, while the previous practice of making an ex-gratia cash payment in cases where members of the private patients plan had to be treated under the NHS was now formalised, guaranteeing substantial 'compensation' to members who found themselves in this position.

Voluntary Hospitals, so now BCWA and the Independent Hospital Group became responsible for helping to develop the new network of private hospitals. BCWA formed a Charitable Trust to distribute funds to charitable private hospitals. This Trust is still very active today; as well as sponsoring a new patients' lounge at St Mary's Hospital and the Physiotherapy wing of the Somerset Nuffield Hospital, it has recently donated, through the National Meningitis Trust, £75,000 towards funding a major three-year research programme into developing a vaccine for meningitis at the University of Surrey, and producing leaflets and information packs for distribution to the public to increase awareness of this life-threatening disease.

Recent years have seen a tremendous increase in the number of people taking out private healthcare. In 1994 BCWA launched two new schemes designed to meet present-day needs;

The following year the Health Services Act (1976) responded to pressure from the medical profession and the health insurers by allowing the private health sector to develop its own facilities. The Independent Hospital Group was set up, with BCWA as one of its founder members; and, just as 50 years earlier BMICS had undertaken to support the

Above: *The Reception Area of Bristol House on Victoria Street in the late 1970s.* **Below:** *The facade of Bristol House to which BCWA moved in 1978 following a period of dramatic expansion.*

THIS STONE WAS LAID BY
MR. P. M. JAMES
CHAIRMAN
Bristol Contributory Welfare Association Ltd
22nd APRIL 1996

information technology and additional staff permit a more rapid and informed response to enquiries. The following year the Associations trading name changed to BCWA Healthcare.

As BCWA Healthcare, the Association will continue to operate as a non-profitmaking organisation, in line with its philanthropic origins; this means that it exists exclusively to serve its members' interests, with any surpluses used not to pay shareholders but to enhance benefits, keep contribution rates low, improve levels of service and increase reserves. It will enter the new millennium firmly committed to retaining and reinforcing its reputation as a 'safe haven' for all, in an increasingly volatile environment.

Preferential Cover meets in full the cost of private specialist investigations and treatment and gives members access to the highest level of facilities and finest standards of treatment and care, while Vital Cover also meets the full cost of in-patient and day-patient treatment for a lower outlay. Confident Dental Healthcare, introduced in 1996, covers the cost of dental treatment. These schemes, based on BCWA's long experience as one of the oldest insurers specialising solely in health insurance, offer outstanding value for money to members, and the Association has always been renowned for its excellent levels of customer service, its simple claims procedure and its helpful, efficient and sympathetic staff.

Top left: Alan Tasker, Deputy Chairman, laying the foundation stone for James Tudor House in 1996.
Top right: The completed James Tudor House.
Bottom left: Sarah Marshall, Roz Murdoch and Philip Fowles promoting BCWA at an exhibition in Harrogate in 1994. *Below:* Sponsoring the new patients lounge at St. Mary's.

In 1995 BCWA celebrated its Diamond Anniversary with preparations to move to its new offices in James Tudor House, where modern

Excellence always on tap

One thing which the people of Bristol take for granted, as we approach the end of the 20th century, is a plentiful supply of good, clean water. Over a million people depend on Bristol Water for their daily needs, with households and businesses in Bristol, Somerset, Gloucestershire and Wiltshire consuming between them a staggering 320 million litres a day. Water plays an important role in our leisure activities, too; each year some 200,000 people visit Chew Lake where they can go sailing, fish for trout, or simply explore the nature trails and do a spot of birdwatching. And Blagdon Pumping Station and Visitor Centre, with its historic beam pumping engines, attracts a further 25,000 visitors a year, including many school parties. Bristol is fortunate: it lies amongst the beautiful Mendip Hills which supply both Blagdon and Chew Lake, it has the river Severn flowing near it, and nowadays it has Bristol Water to treat and distribute its water; so we might be rather at a loss today to understand the grim humour which caused the locals to joke, in the early 19th century, that they preferred to drink Bristowe Beer - because it was safer than water.

Their problem was that although they had the Mendip Hills and the Severn, they did not have Bristol Water. Instead they had a waterworks system composed of conduits and wells unchanged since medieval times, and the water it

Right: The Hotwells Tunnel construction in the 1930s. The men are grouting behind the steel lining.
Below: The Hotwells Tunnel goes under the Avon Estuary (its route taking it right under the Clifton Suspension Bridge).

delivered was polluted and dangerous and liable to give them cholera, dysentry and typhoid. Several localised attempts were made to improve the situation, but none faced up to the fact that Bristol, at the time the country's second most important port city with some 130,000 inhabitants, needed a far-reaching scheme to supply the whole of the city; none, that is, until a set of radical plans was put forward by a group of Bristol citizens, met with general approval and resulted in the formation, by Act of Parliament on 16th July 1846, of the Bristol Waterworks Company.

The twelve directors appointed under the Act included one gentleman, four men whose occupations are not specified, physician William Budd (one of the exponents of the germ theory and sanitation), and five traders, including choco-

reservoirs on the outskirts of Bristol, bringing fresh clean water within the reach of the whole of Bristol. This triumph of Victorian engineering, the Line of Works, is 16 kilometers long with a conduit 30 inches in diameter, and is still in use today.

Today, Bristol Water takes water from 68 different sources: reservoirs, rivers, springs, wells and boreholes. The River Severn is the largest single source, with the Sharpness Canal acting as an open air water main capable of supplying more than half the daily needs of Bristol Water's customers, while 30,000 million litres of Mendip water are stored in Blagdon Reservoir (opened in 1901) and Chew Lake (opened in 1956). Water from these various sources is treated at 23 treatment works, with the water from a difficult lowland source such as the Severn requiring much more complex treatment than the purer water from the Mendip reservoirs. Once the water has been treated, it is stored at 140 covered service reservoirs

latier Francis Fry. Capital of £200,000 was raised by 8,000 shares at £25 each. A plan had been devised to draw supplies from three major sources: the Cold Bath Springs at Barrow Gurney, the spring at Harptree Coombe, and the Watery Coombe springs at Chewton Mendip; this involved ducting the water over valleys and through tunnels under hills, but within little more than a year an aqueduct had been built to carry water from the Mendip springs to giant

Top: *In the days when hosepipes were licenced, use was monitored by the Bristol Waterworks Field Inspection Team. Here we see a typical check.*
Left: *The BWW Transport fleet until December 1951.*

located at strategic points. The whole network is linked by 6,470 kilometers of mains, ranging in diameter from 50mm to 1200mm, and water is kept flowing by some 164 remote-controlled pumping stations - although in some areas it has been possible to site the Works in such a position that gravity alone is sufficient to keep the water flowing.

Maintaining and improving this extensive network is a challenge which Bristol Water has met with impressive efficiency over the years. The temperamental British weather poses perennial problems to water suppliers; very early in its history the company had to contend with the terrible drought of 1864 when Mendip springs dried to a trickle, and readers will remember a number of hot, dry summers more recently which have tested the efficiency of the country's water companies and shown Bristol Water to be among the best. It is not only hot summers which create problems, either; a very cold spell in the winter of 1961-62 caused serious frost damage, fracturing 245 mains within a fortnight and leaving 1900 householders requiring assistance with burst pipes. And during the two wars, water

mains sustained damage on 27 occasions, necessitating 399 mains repairs and 3,842 service pipe repairs.

Improvements in more recent years include more than £22million invested in installing the latest treatment technology at the huge Purton Works and at the same time expanding capacity to guarantee the region's water supply well into the next century. A rolling programme of investment ensures that the system continues to work at maximum efficiently; over the last three years a sum of around £60million has been spent on replacing old pipes, laying new ones, building treated water reservoirs and improving treatment works.

Bristol Water has long been recognised as a leader in water industry technology. The company was among the first to introduce computer-aided telemetry to scan the network, and today third generation telemetry computers enable the highly automated system to be

Above: An aerial view of the Purton Treatment Works. Top: The Queen opening Chew Valley Lake (the main Mendip supply lake to Bristol) in April 1956.

monitored round the clock from the central control room. The company also had the first fully operational ozone water treatment plant in daily use in England, and was one of the first water companies to introduce electronic leak correlators and flow modulated pressure control valves. This has resulted in the company having one of the lowest leakage levels in the country; its leakage prevention programme has brought an estimated saving of almost two million litres of water a day, and this achievement has received official recognition in the award of an energy efficiency award. The success in leakage prevention has also decreased the urgency of developing new sources.

A wealth of knowledge, skills and experience lies behind Bristol Water's achievement of the high standards of excellence which have been formally recognised by the award of BS5750 accreditation - it was the first water company to achieve this - and current ISO 9002 certification for all its operations. This expertise enables the company to provide a wide-ranging consultancy service on matters from leakage management to pipeline and plant design; for instance, it was commissioned to act as consultant on a leakage control programme set up as part of a project funded by the World Bank to rehabilitate the water and wastewater systems within Trinidad and Tobago. The Bristol Water Holdings plc umbrella also covers Bristol Water Pipeline Services whose services include commercial irrigation, water treatment and plumbing; Walter Lawrence, a world-wide construction contractor with special expertise in water, gas and oil installations in airport, petrochemical and pharmaceutical environments; and a carbon regeneration plant run as a joint venture with a Dutch company. Further expansion and diversification of these non-core activities in the company's own specialist field, both at home and abroad, are planned for the future.

The company which was set up in response to a desperate need for improved water supplies in Bristol has remained alert to areas of need where it can offer assistance. The WaterAid appeal was launched in 1982 and each year water consumers contribute generously to the scheme; and in 1991 Bristol Water supplied an articulated lorry to join an aid convoy bound for Romania.

However, Bristol Water's primary responsibility remains towards the people of Bristol, and these responsibilities it fulfills with assiduity and dedication. Its nationally-accredited laboratories run an intensive water quality programme which monitors and tests the water at all stages of the treatment and supply process, from source to tap; during a year over 600,000 analyses are carried out, with some 50,000 samples taken from customers' taps. Water quality has improved steadily, with 99.9 per cent of all samples now meeting or bettering the requirements.

Left: A typical school party to one of Bristol Water's sites. Below: The modern use of the Blagdon Pumping Station - it still pumps water and sees 25,000 visitors a year.

A leaf through history

The American Indians were the first to enjoy smoking tobacco, both as a form of relaxation and in its ceremonial usage in the ritual sealing of negotiations with the famous pipe of peace. European explorers picked up the habit and took it home, often to the alarm of the uninitiated; apparently Raleigh's servant, fearing his smoking master to be afire, hurled a bucket of water over him.

Throughout its fascinating history tobacco has been enjoyed in a variety of forms. Snuff, which is tobacco ground to a powder and flavoured with essences, was very popular during the 18th century, when it was taken with considerable elegance and ceremony from plain or ornate and valuable snuff boxes which today are collectors' items. British soldiers in the Peninsula came across cigars - which the Spaniards smoked incessantly - and took them home where they became popular amongst all sections of society from coal heavers to courtiers. Pre-war actors had cigarettes made to order with their monogram printed on the paper - an up-market version of the 'Blue Line' ration cigarettes formerly issued in HM Ships. The original Navy Cut originated when seamen rolled tobacco leaves tightly in a coil of tarry twine and hacked off sections to chew or smoke. At one time fashionable people preferred the exclusivity of the oval-shaped cigarettes containing

Top left: Henry Overton Wills the first who founded the firm in 1786. Right: William Day Wills. Far right: Henry Overton Wills II whose initials and those of his brother William gave the company it's name. Below: The impressive headquarters of WD & HO Wills until 1973.

Turkish or Egyptian tobacco, or even Black Russian cigarettes with gold paper tips, as once smoked by the Czar! Holiday makers in the 1950s came back from France either loving or hating the soft-packed cigarettes made of sharp-flavoured African tobacco. Mild Virginian tobacco has long been the preferred choice of British smokers who regard it as the best leaf from which, in the past, a bewildering catalogue of brands were made by dozens of local tobacco companies scattered around Britain.

It was from an alliance of 13 of these family-run tobacco firms that Imperial Tobacco Ltd was formed in 1901, to prevent James Buchanan Duke, head of the giant American Tobacco Company, from monopolising British processing and marketing. The first chairman of the new consolidation was Sir William Henry Wills Bt., later Lord Winterstoke. Sir William also owned the family tobacco firm established in Bristol by Henry Overton Wills in 1786. Henry Overton Wills, originally from a Salisbury clock-making family, had come to Bristol at the age of 25 and formed Wills, Watkins & Co in partnership with a Mr Watkins, operating from premises at 73 Castle Street until 1791, when they joined forces with Peter Lilly and moved to Redcliffe Street. By 1789 Mr Watkins had retired and the company had been

renamed Wills & Co; it became W D & H O Wills after the founder's death in 1826, when his two sons William Day Wills and Henry Overton Wills the Second jointly took over an expanding family business, now also estab-

lished in Mary-le-Port Street. In 1865 the company set up a factory in London. By that time cigarette manufacture was already mechanised to some extent, although most of the harvesting and preparation of the tobacco leaf, which was packed in casks or hogsheads

weighing 885 pounds and brought across the Atlantic by steamer, was still done by hand. The first Robert Legg cutting machine had been introduced in 1859, and in 1883 Harry Wills acquired the revolutionary Bonsack cigarette-making machine which could produce 200 cigarettes a minute, slashing production costs and leading to the introduction of the 'Wild Woodbine', still made today.

In 1886 manufacturing began at Bristol in what became known as the No. 1 factory, in East Street, Bedminster. Designed by Frank Wills and described by the Press as 'the finest and most complete tobacco factory in the United Kingdom', the factory's accommodation typified the company's caring attitude towards its employees. Each department had its own dining room and kitchen, and the 2000 employees enjoyed good working conditions, annual outings and, from 1891, annual paid holidays.

Further factories were set up at Ashton Gate and Raleigh Road, and after the formation of The Imperial

*Top right: Sir William Henry Wills (later Lord Winterstoke), who became the first chairman of Imperial Tobacco. **Left:** An early advertisement for Wild Woodbine cigarettes, still made today. **Below:** A Bonded Warehouse at Canon's Marsh, Bristol, where tobacco would be stored until required whereupon a duty would be paid to the Customs and Excise authorities upon withdrawal.*

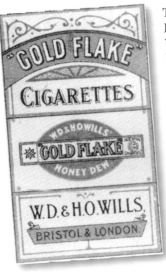

Tobacco Company Limited, with W D & H O Wills and Nottingham-based John Player & Sons as its main shareholders, manufacturing also took place in Swindon, Belfast, Glasgow and Newcastle. The following year Imperial Tobacco acquired Ogdens' pipe tobacco and cigarette plant in Liverpool.

By the time of World War I Imperial Tobacco was well established, and had just launched the Embassy brand which continues to be a best-seller today. Many employees were engaged in military service - their names are listed on the company's Roll of Honour and the War Service Roll - and the Swindon factory became a munitions factory between 1916 and 1919. Cigarette production continued, although the many cigarette-card collectors would have been disappointed that the cards were withdrawn between 1917 and 1922 due to shortage of materials. Post-war cigarette consumption fell initially during the depression, but then increased steadily from 1924 onwards to reach 200 million pounds (weight) in 1938. The second world war brought more disappointment to cigarette cards fans, as these were again withdrawn, this time never to reappear. Again, cigarettes continued to be available, albeit in paper packets, and the filter-tipped brands which were introduced in 1949 to conserve leaf and offer an economy to smokers have remained in demand to this day.

During the 1960s Imperial Tobacco began to diversify into food, drink and leisure, purchasing companies such as the HP Sauce Group, Golden Wonder, Smedleys and Courage Ltd, and in 1973 the company was renamed Imperial Group Ltd to reflect this change of direction, while Imperial Tobacco Ltd was formed to handle

tobacco products. The 1970s brought difficult trading conditions for the tobacco industry; the oil crisis wreaked havoc with the economy, and Britain's entry into the Common Market resulted in tax changes which made king size cigarettes more attractive than the small filter cigarettes which were Imperial's main product. In 1977 Imperial closed its London factory.

Profitability was restored in the 1980s, however, and in April 1986 the food, drink and leisure element of the business was sold off, leaving the Imperial Tobacco Group to concentrate once more on its tobacco interests. Its mission today is to remain focused on tobacco and tobacco-related products only, to strengthen its market position in the UK and Europe, and to improve productivity and control costs through

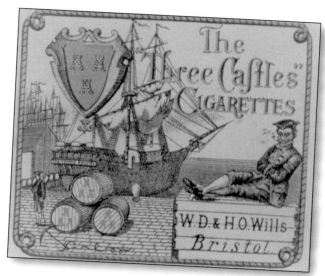

investment in new technology and product design. A century ago W D & H O Wills were right at the forefront of production technology, and today Imperial Tobacco occupies the same position; the last few years have seen investment in ultra high-speed cigarette making and packing complexes, capable of producing 14,000 cigarettes per minute, while cigars are made by high-speed over rolling machines which wrap the outer leaf spirally around the cigars at the rate of up to 400 sticks per minute.

With its UK market share currently standing at some 38 percent, Imperial Tobacco's products fall into five categories: cigarettes, cigars, pipe tobacco and snuff, roll-

Top left: *Gold Flake Cigarettes.*
Above: *The famous Three Castles brand of cigarette.* **Left:** *A view of the cigarette making room around the turn of the 20th Century.*

your-own tobacco and cigarette papers. Cigarette brands include Embassy, Regal, Lambert and Butler, Superkings, JPS, and older brands such as Woodbine and Capstan; Bristol, the very first cigarette brand, launched in 1871 and originally made by hand, was withdrawn in 1974. Today's cigar smokers can choose from Castella, Classic, Panama and King Edward Coronet, while the current range of loose tobaccos includes Golden Virginia, Drum, St Bruno and Gold Block. Rizla, the world's largest producer and marketer of cigarette papers, became part of Imperial Tobacco in 1997.

From the founding of H O Wills in 1786 right up to 1969, when Christopher Wills retired from the post of Sales Research Manager, there was always at least one member of the Wills family involved in the business. In all some 30 members of the family, representing five generations, have served the company. The family's,

and company's, connections with Bristol, too, have always been strong. W H Wills, Sir George Wills and Dr Kenneth were Sheriffs of Bristol; and there can be few charities or welfare organisations within the city which have not benefited from the Wills family's munificence. It was a Wills donation that founded Bristol University, and the University's Wills Tower, containing 'Great George', the fourth largest bell in England, is one of the city's greatest architectural reminders of the Wills family. The family's financial support of the University, amounting to some £2 million over the years, has been responsible for much of its development and expansion. The survival of the oldest theatre in the country, the Theatre Royal, and the restoration of St Mary Redcliffe in 1954 also owe much to the philanthropic generosity of the Wills family. Bristol remains, too, one of the company's manufacturing bases, providing secure and valued employment for the local people; all cigars are made at Winterstoke Road, while cigarette production takes place in Nottingham.

While Imperial Tobacco continues to develop its international presence, with sales in over 70 counties in Europe and the Middle East accounting for more than a quarter of its profits, we in this country will always regard Imperial Tobacco, its founding family and its products as part of our culture and heritage. To the UK's 15 million smokers, Imperial Tobacco is a tobacco giant, and to the inhabitants of Bristol the Wills family is an important benefactor. The company and its founders have even found their way into English literary tradition: Thackeray immortalised Three Castles cigarettes (first made by W D & H O Wills in 1878) in his novel 'The Virginian', while J B Priestley wrote in his English Journey in 1934, "Among the best examples of people activated by civic pride are the members of the Wills family . . . They have chosen to remain in Bristol, the city that made their fortunes for them, and they have spent enormous sums of money in the place." There can be no greater tribute.

Top left: King Edward VII and Queen Mary during a visit to the factory.
Left: The East Street, Bedminster factory and the familiar clock in the 1970s.
Below: Imperial Tobacco's current Bristol headquarters.

Family values and experience in motoring matters

The land alongside the main Bristol to Weston-super-Mare road through Cambridge Batch, where Clist and Rattle's showroom now stands, used to belong to the estate of Lady Smythe. After the end of the first world war two ex-servicemen, brothers-in-law Captain Leslie Clist and Sergeant Sidney Rattle, invested £100 each and bought an acre of land from Lady Smythe, next to what was then the main road between Weston and Bristol. Here, in 1922, they built a corrugated iron shed some 36 feet by 24 feet, and set up in business together, repairing things and selling petrol from cans stored at the premises. Leslie was an electrical engineer and Sidney, the son of an engineer at Yatton Water Works, was a fully-qualified mechanical engineer, having served a complete seven-year apprenticeship. Sidney was a keen motorcyclist, and was to travel to work and back for many years on his 1902, belt-driven, Belgian-made FN motor cycle. The two men began by mending bicycles and miscellaneous electrical items, then progressed to motorbike and car repairs, and in 1923 they started a car hire business, acting as chauffeurs to the local landed gentry.

Their enterprise paid off; by 1925 they had amassed enough capital to build a proper garage and workshop, with underground petrol storage tanks and a generator to provide electricity. A period of expansion followed; for a time they ran a second business at Potters Hill, Felton, and the Cambridge Batch site was developed still further with the construction of two houses at the back of the garage and a cafe next to it. Leslie and Sidney's wives, Lilian Clist and Dorothy Rattle, used the houses to provide bed and breakfast accommodation for travellers and also for some of the students at nearby Long Ashton Research

Top: Leslie and Lilian Clist. **Right:** *Mr Clist in his chauffeur's uniform.* **Below:** *The original premises.*

station, while the cafe became a well-known landmark in the district and an ideal place for local people to meet and enjoy a meal or a snack. Lilian and Dorothy's home-made cakes, fruit drinks and ice-cream became legendary throughout the area.

In the early 1930s Messrs Clist and Rattle were the talk of Bristol's motorists when they became the first garage on the Weston Road to have electrically-operated petrol pumps installed. An article in 'Town and Country News' dated 30th December 1932 was most enthusiastic about their 'six illuminated petrol pumps and several oil bins, carrying the popular brands of petrols and lubricating oils, and also a free air-service point.' By this time the workshop, too, was equipped with all the latest technology of the day, including a Tecalemit Service Station with a hydraulic ramp, Black & Decker decarbonising and valve refacing plant, cylinder grinding plant incorporating honing and boring bar, lathe and general machine shop tools, and other up-to-date plant and equipment, with compressed air points installed throughout. In 1934 a new car showroom was opened, but at the same time the cafe closed, giving Lilian and

Dorothy a well-earned rest but depriving the locals of the home-made cakes of which they had become so fond.

As trade increased, largely as a result of the personal recommendations of satisfied customers, each partner began to specialise in his own side of the business. Car sales were handled by Leslie Clist; the firm had been appointed Austin dealers in 1928, but the firm could supply any make of car and dealt in both new and second-hand vehicles. Repair work, for which the garage held official RAC and AA approval, was supervised by Sidney Rattle as works foreman. They were assisted by Mr Victor Gill, who joined the firm in its very early days and stayed with them for over 50 years, later becoming reception engineer and service manager. The firm also stocked a full range of spares and accessories, and operated a breakdown service using a fully-equipped breakdown van with towing and lifting facilities.

In 1938 disaster struck: fire broke out in the engine house at the back of the premises, and spread rapidly. Sidney Rattle's son Bob spotted the flames and raised the alarm; the men tried to keep the fire in check with buckets of water and a hose, while passing motorists obligingly stopped and helped move nearly 40 cars to safety away from the flames. By the time the fire brigade arrived the engine house was burning furiously; the firemen managed to stop the blaze spreading to the main garage premises and to the 1,000 gallons of crude oil stored close to the engine house, but the engine house itself together with the generating plant, compressors, switchboards and other equipment was totally destroyed. Two vehicles belonging to Clist and Rattle were damaged, and the fire spread to adjoining

Top: The original workshop with Mr Rattle standing alongside the car and Mr Clist in the background. Above: The teashop and garage pictured in 1920. Right: The Fire Station premises at the back of the garage, 1942.

premises, gutting Messrs Bast's cabinetmaking works and van, and a shed and contents belonging to a coal merchant, Mr J White, before it was finally brought under control. The total cost of the damage amounted to in excess of £2,000. However, within 24 hours power had been restored thanks to a borrowed generator, and some three months later new buildings had been erected to replace those destroyed in the fire. Later that year, Mr Clist became superintendant of the Long Ashton RDC Fire Brigades.

The next challenge came in the form of the second world war. Part of garage site became a base for the auxilliary fire service, and half the workshop was given over to the war effort, being used for storage and for round-the-clock production of parts for tanks. Sidney Rattle supervised the war work and carried on running the business in the limited space that was left.

As things returned to normal after the war, Clist and Rattle continued to develop their reputation for reliable, honest trading. Over the years they continued to supply a full range of cars including Austin, Morris, Wolseley,

Riley, Triumph, Standard and Ford. New petrol pumps were installed, two acres of land to the rear of the premises were acquired for development, and the next generation began to lend a hand; Leslie Clist's sons Peter and Richard became involved in running the firm, taking over when first Sidney Rattle and then Leslie Clist retired from the business they had founded some thirty years earlier.

In response to a growing demand for accident repair work, a large new panel beating and bodywork department, equipped with the latest facilities to undertake work for the leading insurance companies and repair accident-damaged vehicles to a high standard, was opened during the 1960s. Plans for the new Long Ashton by-pass then began to cast some doubts over the future of the Cambridge Batch Garage, as there were fears that passing trade would be lost, and when construction began on the by-pass the company acquired Ettrick Garage at Backwell. Clist and Rattle reached its 50th

Top and above: *Mr Clist is pictured greeting customers at the launch of the new showroom in 1938.*

anniversary in 1972 and celebrated half a century's service to the motoring public at both Cambridge Batch and Ettrick Garage. Motorists visiting the company's new forecourt shop at that time could have bought a gallon of Essolube 30 oil for 65p, or for those who were saving Green Shield Stamps, a special promotion on Uniflo oil offered a quarter of a book of Green Shield Stamps free with every gallon tin. It became apparent that fears over the adverse effects of the by-pass had been unfounded; petrol sales at Cambridge Batch remained good, and happily the company was able to retain its original premises. Ettrick Garage was subsequently disposed of, but the company continued to operate from two sites as on 1st June 1973 it took over Portishead Service Station in High Street, from where they operated a Morris franchise. During this era, customers looking for a new car could go to Cambridge Batch to check out the Austin range which consisted of the Austin Mini, the Allegro or the Maxi - over Easter 1974 a one-year old, M-registered Maxi 1750 with 9000 miles on the clock, cost new £1525, was on offer at £1195 - or they could visit Portishead to inspect the exciting new Marina range, while those looking for something sportier might have wanted to test-drive the Mini Clubman or even the MGB GT.

Motoring has changed a lot since those days, but Clist and Rattle today is one of the few family firms still operating in the motor trade under the ownership and control of the family which founded it. Peter Clist, the Chairman, is based at Cambridge Batch Rover dealership, while the newly-refurbished Renault franchise at Portishead is run by Managing Director Paul Clist, Peter's son. At both its branches the firm offers the motoring public a friendly and obliging service, combining a 'no-pressure' sales policy with a 'one-stop shop' approach, offering a full range of after-sales service, routing servicing and repairs, parts and accessories and vehicle hire. With a reputation built on trust and customer care and a wealth of experience which is second to none, Clist and Rattle's aim is to provide the same high level of service which Bristol's motorists have come to expect from this family firm.

Top: *The garage pictured in the early 1970s.* ***Left:*** *A 1990s view of the same premises.* ***Below:*** *The 'A' Team, from left to right, John Collins, After Sales Director, Paul Clist, Managing Director, Lyn Jones, Receptionist, Peter Clist, Chairman and Jonathan Hart, Sales Director, pictured during a Castrol Competition.*

The fastest baycarts-carriages charabancs-trucks-vans-artics in the West

It is perhaps not so surprising that one of Bristol's major haulage companies should have developed out of the spare-time activities of a busy Brislington farmer. Farmers, after all, own tractors and trailers and spend a fair proportion of their time transporting goods from one bit of land to another and bringing in supplies from further afield; which, after all, is what hauliers do, though perhaps on a rather different scale. However, when Farmer C F Russett took the first steps towards

establishing Pioneer Haulage, the company which was to be the forerunner Premier Transport, it was still horses and carts, not tractors and trailers, that carried his goods; in fact, he was famous for his comment that he 'didn't think mechanical contrivances would catch on.'

During the 1880s Farmer Russett was approached by the local sawmills to collect their sawdust, and at first he used to spread it on his fields to get rid of it. This seemed to him to be a waste, so he then began separating the sawdust into coarse and fine. He sold the coarse to slaughterhouses, and the fine to butchers' shops, which proved a very satisfactory solution all round and especially for Farmer Russett. Encouraged by the success of this little venture, he began to develop other services, offering amongst other things a seven-day delivery service to London using his teams of horses. By 1921 he had changed his opinion of 'mechanical contrivances' sufficiently to go so far as to buy a very fine contraption which he could operate as a

Below: One of Pioneer's early trucks in 1921.

motorised truck during the week and convert to a charabanc at weekends; his son Harold's (H.E.) wife used to enjoy driving their fare stage bus from Keynsham to Bristol.

C F Russett's Pioneer Haulage empire continued growing until 1936, when the business was divided up between his eight sons, with H.E. Russett inheriting the Parcel division which he ran until 1946. His son, also Harold (H.A.) took over the business after the untimely death of his father just a few days after returning home from Germany following the second world war. H A. Russett continued running the Parcel division until nationalisation took over in 1949, whereupon he was made divisional manager of the new British Road Services.

When denationalisation arrived just five years later H.A. Russett

Top Left: *A family photo from the early part of the 20th century, the founder C F Russett is seated in the centre of the front row, Harold Senior is standing third from the left on the back row and Harold Junior is on the far left of the middle row.* **Left:** *The Premier Transport Fleet pictured in 1957.* **Below:** *An Armstrong Sawer 1932 lorry passing 48 Days Road in 1938.*

members of Palletline, which operates on a 'hub and spoke' system, setting up district depots so that small, regional, family businesses could operate on a national scale. In its first night 51 pallets were handled. Today there are 44 depots, handling 10,000 pallets every 24 hours.

In 1998 Premier was sold to Gregory Distribution but Bob Russett still continues the family involvement in the transport industry with his role as Chairman of Palletline PLC.

Left: Harold A Russett pictured with his wife Grace, son Bob and daughter Judith outside Buckingham Palace following his investiture in 1984.
Below: A 1934 Leyland Beaver belonging to Premier passing the Guildhall in London during the Cart Marking Ceremony. This ceremony is open to Freemen of the City of London and harks back to the days before Road Tax when haulage transport would be given different 'mark' each year following payment of taxes.
Right: A modern day Premier Transport lorry carrying the Palletline livery.

bought six vehicles and restarted Premier Transport as a parcels carrier, his wife Grace was an important factor in helping to run the business and her roles ranged from keeping the books to unloading lorries. Since then, the company has continued to grow and the family has made a tremendous contribution to the haulage industry. The family became involved in the Road Haulage Association since it was founded in 1945 and since then there has always been a Russett on the National Council. Both H.A. Russett, his uncle Frank and his son Bob have served as National Council Members for the RHA; Harold was the RHA Natonal Chairman between 1982 and 1984, and received the OBE in 1984 for services to transport.

Also in 1984 he became the President of the Bristol Chamber of Commerce, and still in that same year Bob was made Freeman of London, an honour which had been bestowed on his father in 1972.

Bob had taken over the running of Premier in 1982, and by 1988 the business had grown so large that he decided to sell off the parcels side of it to City Transport. This left Premier to concentrate on pallet freight and distribution, and on 1st February 1992 it became one of the four founder

Fish as fresh as a sea breeze

Do you remember when everyone ate fish on Fridays because it was the religious thing not to eat red meat once a week? Almost every town in Britain then had a high street branch of the Scottish company Macfisheries to supply the need. So great was our appetite for fresh fish, the cheapest meat of all thanks to the one time great sea fishing industry, that fishmongers were as common as butchers. Each fish shop was open to the street so that customers could see, and smell, the artistically displayed array of fish, and game too, which glistened on sloping marble slabs. Modern health officials would blanch at the thought of such an unhygienic practice and yet we thrived on it, unlike the illness prone folk reared in a more protected environment.

Times change and still some will recall the Bristol fishmongers Bigwoods, of Baldwin Street hard by St Nicholas Fish Market, who were bought up by Macfisheries in their era of expansion. Those were the days when the Macfisheries annual diaries provided customers with a different fish or game recipe for every day of the year. The Bigwoods branches were renamed Charles Saunders and it was in these that Chris Scott, the present Managing Director, learned his trade. Anyone who has gutted and dressed fish will recognise the skills, once practiced by legendary fishwives, that make light work of a task many prefer to leave to others.

It was in the all important buying, storing and handling of goods which can be so easily damaged and become poisonous when past their sell by date that Chris Scott excelled. His abilities were recognised in a market where reputation is all important and rewarded by promotion until he became the Regional Manager for the company which was by then known as Macfish. Fresh fish stored in refrigerators and displayed on layers of crushed ice was rapidly becoming replaced by convenient packs of frozen fish. These suit the modern style of living and indeed of catering, both in institutions and hotels, where boneless, skinless cuts of fish can be cooked with the minimum of time consuming preparation and no waste.

In 1983 Chris Scott bought the Charles Saunders fresh fish wholesale and retail enterprise from Macfisheries. As an independent trader with an eye to the future he put into practice a modernisation scheme which concentrated on the frozen fish side of the business. He moved to purpose built premises in St Philips equipped with the latest cold storage facilities. The frozen fish share of the market has grown from 60% of total fish sales to around 80%, which explains why there are fewer fresh fishmongers to be found on the high streets of Britain. Those who enjoy preparing and cooking glistening pearly

Below: *The Bigwood store in Baldwin Street in 1907.*

fish to suit all palates and pockets from retailers like Charles Saunders.

Charles Saunders are proud of their ability to obtain an extensive range of top quality fresh fish and sea food to offer to their discerning customers. There is no doubt that foreign travel and the fascinating TV cookery programmes have tickled the British palate to explore

skinned fresh fish no longer have to catch their own, however, as it is becoming easier to obtain a range of

Above: Mac Fisheries pictured during the 1930s.
Below: The original shop in Baldwin Street, dressed for Christmas 1960.

beyond old favourites such as cod and haddock. To cater for the exploding national interest in the joys of cooking and eating the firm stocks an astonishing variety of over 2,000 lines of speciality frozen foods. Try counting the ones you know and see what untried treats lie in store for the adventurous cook.

It was once considered dangerous to eat shellfish in a month without an R in it. Thanks to freezing these delicacies can be enjoyed at any time while frozen crab sticks may replace the once popular pint of cockles, after all what happens if the eater has lost their pin? The once ubiquitous Prawn Cocktail, served at every dinner dance, was only possible in mass catering thanks to the fish freezing industry, before that it was either an expensive luxury or a treat restricted to the appropriate seaside areas.

Country dwellers in the not so distant past could only eat sea fish with any degree of safety if it had been salted to preserve it. This was replaced by packing fish in ice but even so any delays in delivery or cooking could lead to unhappy rural tummies. Frozen fish has changed all this so that village housewives can find, and safely stock, the more popular lines from their local shops. It is hard to recall that many villagers relied on oil lamps and bottled gas operated cookers, and the rarer gas refrigerators, until electricity was brought to them in the years following World War II.

The Charles Saunders catchment area covers a radius of sixty miles around Bristol so that those living in the towns and villages in the counties of

Avon, Devon, Gloucestershire and Somerset can rely on the best of frozen foods. These are delivered by state of the art refrigerated vehicles from processing plants around the coast so that the sea food products are kept frozen from factory to kitchen table. Such high standards are maintained by the firm's own quality inspectors under the overall eye of various public health officials. A far cry from the days when stinking fish was sold off cheaply as the unrefrigerated shops of the gas light era put up their shutters for the night.

As so many people eat out today, what with youngsters browsing on the latest style of school meals and 'take away' cooked food shops replacing other retailers in smaller shopping centres, the catering element of Charles Saunders has grown to meet demand. Contracts for fully prepared frozen foods for schools and hospitals, works canteens and cafes, pubs and restaurants are vital to the trade of a large wholesaler. The value added element of preparation is tremendously important to cost conscious catering concerns paying high rents and rates for premises. Limited space can be devoted to tables and chairs for customers instead of preparation and segregated fresh food storage facilities in the kitchen area. The skilled staff can spend all their time on

cooking instead of coming in hours earlier to prepare raw foods.

Today the skilled practitioners of food preparation work in the kitchens of the food processors to provide professional caterer and housewife alike with well prepared dishes from around the world. All that the busy part-time housewife, with a full time career beyond the home, needs to do is select a package or two of conveniently prepared frozen food, pop it into a microwave, and 'hey presto' the meal is ready. The happy band of 'food freaks', ranging from husbands helping out or showing off as weekend chefs to people with a genuine love of the culinary arts, find frozen foods a valuable addition to their armoury of talent, store cupboard and fresh produce.

There is no doubt that the forward thinking firm established with such success by Chris Scott is alive to the potential of every corner of the cookery field. There are now thirteen refrigerated vehicles maintaining supplies to every user of their healthy, tasty range of products. It has been widely accepted that freezing is the best way of preserving the taste, and the all important nutritional value, of a wide range of foods ever since Antarctic explorers first

tucked into cans of food left behind by their predecessors. The National Health Service relies on Charles Saunders to maintain the quality and variety required by patients throughout the region.

In 1995 Charles Saunders was invited to participate in the development of the quality award scheme run by the Sea Fish Industry Authority and was the first company to win the ISO 9002. The firm is also a member of the British Frozen Food Federation and one of the largest of the twenty members of the Fairways Frozen Foods buying consortium. This group distributes frozen foods produced by brand leaders, such as Charles Saunders, under the Fairway label, itself a guarantee of top quality frozen food. Charles Saunders plans to build extensive cold storage facilities to cope with an increase in market share in the new millennium. The company provides a first class service giving local customers the backing of an organisation with national purchasing power.

Left: An early view of James Bigwood's store.
Above: Jon Wright, left and Chris Scott second left, receive their BS5750 certificate from the Lord and Lady Mayoress of Bristol. *Below:* Just some of the Charles Saunders delivery fleet.

An Englishman's home is his castle

In the mid 19th century the thriving inland port of Bristol was beginning to lose its place as the Second City in the kingdom to the Northern industrial cities, as they grew from clusters of villages, and to the more easily accessible port of Liverpool. Bristol's population of 140,000 was served by two MPs, a lord mayor, two sheriffs and were housed in 18,000 dwelling houses. The unfortunate homeless poor were kept in four uncomfortable workhouses whose regime was so discouraging that only the desperate sought parish relief. On the benefit side Income Tax was 7d (3p) in the pound and a ton of best Welsh coal cost 11/6d (58p) when untaxed farm workers and soldiers earned 7s (35p) a week.

In order to finance home purchases by working people the local Friendly Societies, formed in the late 18th Century to provide sickness and funeral benefits, initiated the funding of self help building projects. Many of these early societies limited their scope to helping a small group to pay for costs of materials until every member was housed, after which the society was wound up and any surplus funds were shared out among the new houseowners.

In the Bristol Mercury of 22nd June 1850 the newly formed Bristol, West of England and South Wales Permanent Benefit Building Society advertised £100 shares and £50 half shares. These seemingly unaffordable shares were available to clerks and skilled artisans from 4s 3d (21p) a week upwards. By using the joint strength of their local building society the sober and thrifty members of the lower middle classes, earning less than 15s (75p) a week, were able to aspire to comfortable homes costing around £100. Live-in shop assistants were commonplace in the Edwardian era and were often required to work long hours six days a week.

The management of the society was guided by reputable Bristolians of the calibre of the Quaker Fry family, the Caves, Dangers, Cartwrights, Tribes and Whitwills. John Lucas, the first secretary, served for 30 years while secretary C J Lowe and director Sir Frank Wills, the tobacco magnate, were equally prominent as Lord Mayors. The Bristol & West, like other building societies, had grown in stature, wealth and power by the time of the 1874 Building Societies Act. Twenty years later the vexing question of charging Income Tax on member's interest earnings was resolved by making such income exempt from tax. In the last decade of Queen Victoria's reign the society lent £50,000 pa, paid out bonuses which averaged £1,500 pa, and held assets of over £300,000.

A year after the end of the Great War the society held reserves of nearly £64,000 and it advanced loans of £189,830, three times the number of mortgages granted in 1900. The housing market was booming as wartime marriages had increased the post war demand to an estimated 350,000 houses. By the year 1927 the society had assets worth £1 million at a time when even the most spacious suburban and country homes rarely topped £5,000 in value. The name was shortened by cutting the words South Wales Permanent. More than £400,000 had been lent on the English side of the Bristol Channel and the society was doing well. Under the direction of Hubert Bonning it became one of the leading societies in the West Country.

The national building society movement was regarded as a major factor in enabling

Top left: *Mr John Lucas, first chairman of the Society from 1850 to 1880.* ***Above:*** *The Society's first newspaper advertisement that appeared on the front page of The Bristol Mercury on Saturday June 22nd 1850.*

capital, and the half-yearly
dividends and interest to
investors have always been
regularly paid'. Mr Bonning had
resigned in 1948 to be replaced
by Andrew Breach as General Manager who took
over a society which operated from its head office
and just two branches at Bedminster and Bishopton,
suburbs of Bristol. Fifteen years later, under the
guidance of Andrew Breach, there were some 30

*Top left: Staff in the Accounts Department in the
early 1960s. **Top right:** Mr Andrew Breach who
became General Manager of the Bristol & West in 1950
and was chairman of the Building Societies Association
from 1963-1965. **Below:** A mortgage advisor discusses
a loan with a young couple in the late 1950s.*

ordinary people to own their own homes as shown
by inter-war figures for Bristol. Of the 36,000
homes built in Bristol 20,000 were privately owned,
the rest being on the new council estates. The
greatest concentration of new housing was in the
vicinity of the huge aircraft works at Filton and
around the heavily industrialised Avonmouth Docks.
Mortgage holders not only buy or build new houses
they also buy vast numbers of second hand houses.

Many home owners who prefer the size, locations
and character of older houses have found that the
Bristol & West did not follow other societies in
restricting loans to housing stock built within living
memory. Indeed there are many older houses of
charm and interest which have been purchased by
more than one borrowing member of the society.

By the outbreak of World War II the expanding
society, then worth £4 million including reserves of
almost a quarter million pounds, had moved into St
Stephen's House. This, although badly scarred by
the air raids which devastated much of the town
centre, survived the war years in which investments
outpaced loans. The enormous post war housing
shortage, caused partly by enemy action whose
victims required new homes and partly by young
couples no longer content to start their marriages as
paying guests in their in-law's home, was exacer-
bated by the continued rationing of building
materials, petrol and transport. Once these
hampering restrictions were lifted the money
invested during the war by optimistic members was
put to good use as shown by the 1945 loans figure of
half a million rising by 1950 to £1,333,000 out of
total assets of £5 million.

After a century of trading the society could proudly
announce that 'no investor has lost one penny of his

branch offices ranging, initially in the country of the Bristol based former Great Western Railway, from Truro in the west to Royal Tunbridge Wells in the east and from Birmingham in the Midlands to Southampton on the English Channel.

During this era of expansion between 1950 and 1958 Bristol & West moved from 41st to 19th in size by attracting new investors as well as by absorbing a number of smaller building societies in the West Country. The next few years saw the society listed as enjoying 'trustee' status and then opening several offices in London, where the St Marylebone and Suburban Building Society was taken over. By 1960 total assets were in excess of £28 million, rising five years later to over £60 million at a time when family

*Top: A Board Meeting in the 1960s, Andrew Breach is seated third from left. **Left:** The Bristol & West Building Society new head office on Broad Quay, Bristol prior to completion in January 1968.*

cars could be bought new for five or six hundred pounds.

Following expansion throughout southern England the society re-established its earlier links with the Principality of Wales by opening branches in Cardiff and Newport. The administration of a successful modern business is light years ahead of Bristol & West's early days when pen pushing clerks wrote long hand entries into huge tomes. These Dickensian characters, educated by rote and chanted tables, had the remarkable ability of looking down some 30 entries of pounds, shillings and pence, the latter divided into ha'pennies and farthings and coming up with an almost instantaneous total via mental arithmetic.

Since its early days Bristol & West has updated its office procedure, not to mention the machinery which started with the Victorian 'typewriting machines' and 20th century adding machines. Even in our age of computer links between branches and head office Bristol & West still needs to have 'strong rooms' in which to store the mortgage and house deeds deposited by borrowers. Bristol & West provides savings and investment facilities for customers which enable them to get at their money with far greater ease than in the days when written notice was required for all withdrawals, the details of which were hand entered, with deposits, into member's pass books.

Banks and Building Societies have long been regarded by the investor as a sound investment in which their savings will grow. Many such savers steered clear of the exciting, and sometimes risky, world of the stock market in which minimum investments were beyond their reach. Today, however, many Bristolians can afford such national and international investments. In July 1997, under the leadership of Chief Executive John Burke, Bristol & West became part of the Bank of Ireland Group. Bristol & West has now converted to become a

bank with well over a million customers and assets in excess of £12 billion. To many people living in the West Country, and in Bristol in particular, it still remains a firm favourite as a provider of financial services. At Bristol & West customers are able to invest their money to provide funds for house and holidays, family growth and education and not least in importance to make retirement worth while.

The friendly staff in Bristol & West's offices are trained to advise members on all aspects of mortgages, savings and investments and to answer their questions without bias.

Below: *A 1990s view of the Bristol & West Plc.*

John Hodgson - The driving force

John Hodgson, son of the landlord of the Pilgrim Inn near Bristol Bridge (whose name was also John Hodgson), had grown up in the mid 1800s surrounded by the sights and sounds of the nearby St Nicholas Market.

The hustle and bustle of the market held a real attraction for the young man, and accordingly John took what was to prove a key decision not to follow his father into the licenced trade; instead he started work on one of the market stalls. It was there in St Nicholas Market that he became captivated by a young girl who regularly travelled from the Mendips to the market, where she sold rabbits - a very popular food in Britain right up until the second world war. John and Emma became engaged and eventually tied the knot in St Mary Redcliffe. Eager to become successful, the young couple decided to take a unit in the market, where they sold fruit and vegetables. They had no way of knowing that that single unit rented in 1895 was to be the foundation of the John Hodgson group of companies.

John and Emma's little business took off, and such was their phenomenal success that by 1910 the Hodgsons were incredibly operating six market units as well as having retail shops in Redcliffe Hill and Stapleton Road. In a shrewd move they acquired 150 acres of land at Frenchay a mere six years later, where they set about establishing a market garden. The rhubarb, cabbages and other vegetables they grew there supplied much of the produce for their wholesale business. It was there in Frenchay that the enterprising couple set about constructing specially designed rooms for the express purpose of ripening green bananas. Theirs was the first such facility in the country. The business had proved to be every bit as successful as John and Emma had hoped back in 1895; justifiably proud of what they had achieved over the years they were able to retire in 1939. Unfortunately all the land was compulsorily purchased in 1947 by the local council.

Meanwhile their son, the third John Hodgson, had been learning the trade and in 1928 he and his wife Margaret set up their own banana business as John Hodgson Jnr. A few years later he expanded into Swindon, where in 1935 he opened a second branch

Top right: *The founder of the company going to market by horse and cart with his wife and son in 1896.* **Left:** *Two horseless carts pictured in the 1890s.*

of the business. But war was looming on the horizon, and with the declaration of war with Germany in 1939 everything went pear-shaped for the up-and-coming business. The most difficult and challenging years for John Hodgson Jnr were about to begin.

Bananas represented around 80 percent of their trade, and when imports of the fruit stopped they were hit very badly. It was to be another six years before the first bananas that had been seen since before the war were to arrive from the West Indies; in fact children born during the war had never seen a banana before, and had no idea that they had to peel off the skin before they could eat the fruit!

Another blow quite literally fell when the firm's warehouses on the Welsh Back became victims of a Luftwaffe bomb. It is said that bad luck comes in threes, and the Hodgsons found it to be true when their premises at 49 Baldwin Street were badly damaged by bomb blast.

There was nothing to be done except to go on as best they could, and with courage and determi-

Top: *The founder, his wife and son with one of their early trucks pictured in 1920.*
Right: *The Old Market Street and one of John Hodgson's trucks in 1938.*

nation John and Margaret, together with their right hand man Reg Trevett who joined the firm in 1945, weathered the storm and concentrated on redirecting the business into wholesale fruit and vegetables. Those difficult years were punctuated by Hitler, bankers, non-paying customers, tax inspectors - and the rationing that Britain had to endure for far longer than the duration of the war.

John and Margaret's son Keith, who had signed up for service in the army, joined the firm in 1955 after he left the forces. With Keith as its chairman, the wholesale fruit market acquired 15 acres of land at St Philips Marsh, where a new wholesale fruit centre was built. Keith was able to purchase five units in the market, and acquired a further nine making a total of 14 units. Fifteen thousand square feet of warehousing was purchased nearby to meet the demand for further space. It was from here that the transport business developed, with 30 vehicles distributing produce to supermarkets and warehouses, and making other delivery runs to retailers and wholesale markets around Wales and the south west.

A management buy out of the wholesale business in 1980 enabled Keith Hodgson to concentrate on the transport side, which was prospering in its position near the market in St Philips Marsh. The company

*Top: A John Hodgson banana truck pictured in 1936. **Right**: The company fleet pictured in 1999 totalling 30 vehicles.*

was on track for further diversification, however, when with Neil Adams they started an employment agency for drivers and warehousemen. A specialist department was later added to the service in placing information technology personnel through the Internet, which now trades independently as Falcon Services Ltd.

In 1991, under the guidance of Peter Barrett, who had worked with Keith during the 1960s, the company made important developments in the Birmingham area. The Midland Co-operative Society had 200 outlets around the city, and Hodgsons were designated to service these branches daily with fresh produce, milk, bread and chilled products, with around 80 personnel being

the quality of service it can offer to it's clients, and believes in maintaining a high standard of modern equipment, including the fleet of 30 'chilled' vehicles. The vehicles range from 17 tonne to 38 tonne gvw. Regular checks by the FTA complement the high standard of maintenance and ensure a smooth running round the clock delivery service. Cab telephones give staff back at headquarters a quick and effective means of communication with their drivers in the event of a change of plan or a sudden emergency.

employed in the undertaking. Interestingly, the Co-operative movement remains one of Hodgson's main clients.

Today the companies large teams of experienced employees include office staff, warehousemen and HGV drivers, and a high standard of customer satisfaction is uppermost on their day-to-day agenda. As a demonstration of their commitment to quality all the companies are accredited for ISO 9002. The importance of trained staff was early recognised, and in certain circumstances the staff in key positions are trained directly by the clients they are working with. Reciprocally, the team can today offer technical backup that often gives their customers the extra knowledge they need, and this commitment to giving added value for money that customers do not expect has turned out to be Hodgson's unique selling point.

John Hodgson Ltd has always tried to keep at the forefront of new ideas and methods that enhance

A commitment to keeping abreast of technological advances involved the installation of state-of-the-art computers, and today the smooth running of the daily operation of the business is assured by a sophisticated computer network that encompasses all the order processing and documentation for the major clients, route scheduling and fuel usage.

The next generation of Hodgsons - Adam, Ben and Sarah - has now joined the board of what is proving to be a family firm in the true sense of the word. Together with their customers and loyal staff they look forward to the next stage in the history of the John Hodgson group of companies.

Top: One of the fleet of vehicles pictured in front of one of Bristol's famous landmarks, the Clifton Suspension Bridge.

From pirate to connoisseurs in 200 years

Wines have entered Britain through the port of Bristol since Norman times, though both the wines themselves and the import procedures employed have changed somewhat since then. The wines we enjoy today - particularly those obtained through Averys - are without doubt far superior to those our ancestors drank, although the import methods employed by our ancestors were perhaps more colourful, including as they did privateering and even downright piracy. Although Averys has - as far as we know - always obtained its fine wines by strictly legitimate means, the family is not without pirate connections; it seems likely that the famous 17th century pirate Henry Avery, who operated out of Madagascar, was one of the family. Henry Avery seems to have specialised in diamonds, however, and it was not until a century later that Joseph Avery, thought to

be a descendant of Henry, established the family wine and spirit connection when he joined wholesale wine and spirit importer Lax and Co; and it was Joseph's son John who purchased the small retail wine business and pub, founded in 1793, which was to become Averys.

This business was situated at the cross roads between the bottom of Park Street and Frog Lane. Shortly after John had acquired the business, the town planners of the day decided to construct a bridge to carry Park Street over Frog Lane, and John had the premises rebuilt as the handsome Georgian-style Mauretania building, rather more ornate that its neighbours, which still stands at the bottom of Park Street.

During the second half of the 19th century when John Avery set up in business, wine came to England from a number of sources. Early French wines are known to have derived from Poitiers and Anjou, moving down to Bordeaux during King John's reign; a formal trade agreement with Castile signed in 1466 had marked the beginning of regular traffic with Spain, and Portugal was also a well-established source of supply. The reduction of excise duty on wines as compared to spirits in the 1860s created favourable trading conditions, and Averys prospered, with sales in the pub accounting for a large proportion of their profits. John Avery died in 1882 and left the thriving business to his three sons, John Clarke,

Top: Joseph and Frances Avery with their children Ronald, Joyce and Phyllis. **Above:** *An early Christmas advert for Averys 'Christmas Lunch Selection' of sherry.* **Left:** *Ronald Avery with Cellarman, Teddy Tamlin.*

Edwin and Joseph, who continued to run the firm along much the same lines. However, when John Clarke died in 1919 and Edwin went into semi-retirement, inheritance was more of a problem. None of John's sons was interested in going into the family

business; Edwin's only child was a daughter, and Joe had one son, Ronald, who had gone up to Cambridge to read Natural Sciences at Caius College after serving in the war. Joe insisted on Ronald giving up his studies and coming into the business.

Although forced into a profession which was not of his choosing, Ronald excelled as a wine merchant, and it was he who established Averys as a fine wine specialist. He saw the necessity of visiting, tasting and selecting

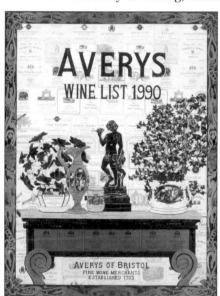

wines at source in order to obtain the best, and in the face of his father's disapproval he proceeded to do just that, skillfully selecting the finest Burgundies and the best vintage Bordeaux wines, and making sure that Averys always had stocks of good vintages to tide over the years when results were disappointing; throughout the 1930s, for instance, when no good vintages were produced, Averys was able to supply its customers with 1929 claret, one of the century's greatest vintages, due to Ronald's foresight in building up stocks. He was also responsible for introducing a wider range of fine wines onto Averys' list, and in short for building up Averys' reputation as a truly distinguished wine merchant.

Ronald's unerring judgement has been passed down to his son John, who has run the company since his father's death in 1976. John has also made the sound business decisions necessary to keep this small family firm ahead of its larger competitors. By forming a partnership, initially with American vintner Clarke Swanson, he increased financial security and investment potential. In 1994 the UK-based wine company Hallgarten Limited replaced Swanson as partners, and since that time the company has relocated to more spacious premises in Nailsea which, unlike the

Park Street warehouse, can accommodate today's large international delivery vehicles.

However, the firm has by no means severed its traditional connections with the Park Street area. In Averys' superb 'Cash and Carry' retail cellar with wonderful brick arches, which opens onto Culver Street, off Frogmore Street and within 100 yards of Park Street, enthusiasts can attend frequent wine tastings to discover some of the world's greatest wines for a very modest sum, or browse through some 1000 wines and buy by the case - twelve bottles of a single wine or twelve different wines - while above this cellar, on Park Street, opposite the Mauretania building, is the new Averys shop where wines are sold by the bottle. Alternatively, many customers elect to use Averys' mail order service, finding the monthly newsletters featuring selected wines a great help in making their choice and can be contacted at Averys of Bristol Limited, Orchard House, Southfield Road, Nailsea, Bristol BS48 1JN, by telephone on 01275 811100 or by fax on 01275 811101.

Begun in 1793, Averys of Bristol has already witnessed the turn of two centuries. As it nears the turn of another century, and the dawn of a new millennium, it has every confidence in the future.

Top left: *Averys former Head Office at the bottom of Park Street.* ***Top right:*** *Averys cellars set up for a tasting.* ***Left:*** *Averys 1990 Wine List created with a montage of just some of their wine labels.* ***Below:*** *John Avery in inspecting the wine in one of his cellars.*

Bristol's modern-day Florence Nightingales

The religious Order which was responsible for founding St Mary's Hospital, The Poor Servants of the Mother of God, was begun in London in 1869. Its foundress, Mother Magdalen Taylor, devoted her life to the service of the sick and the poor, and the Order which she had created carried on this work after her death in 1900. Having already established a number of hospitals, schools and orphanages, the Religious Sisters came to Bristol in 1920. They visited the poor and taught in the Pro Cathedral School, and when numbers 3, 4 and 5 Upper Byron Place became vacant they purchased the property with the intention of setting up a Hospital. Much preparation work was necessary and it was not until 1926, after much preparation work, the hospital was able to take in its first patients.

The hospital was run by the Sisters who all took a share in the various ministries, and facilities included an operating theatre and bed accommodation for 32 patients. Within a few years it was clear that this provision was not adequate. In 1930 a second operating theatre was added and a new X-ray machine installed, and the following year a 30-bed extension was built, so that more patients could benefit from the medical and surgical facilities and the caring ministries of the Sisters in the peaceful surroundings of St Mary's. The war brought difficult and anxious times, however; in 1941 damage to the buildings made it necessary for Sisters and patients to evacuate to Chew Magna, and they were not able to return to Bristol until 1944.

Above and below: *Two aspects of St Mary's Hospital in the late 1920s.*

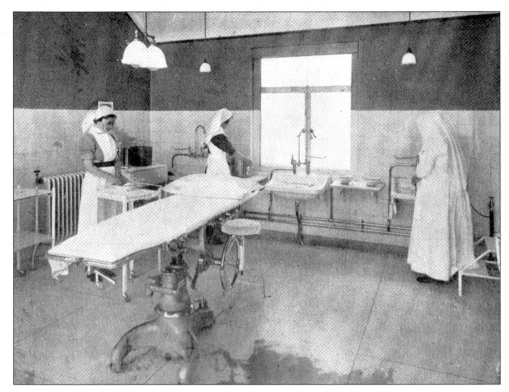

nursing staff and resident doctors who provide 24-hour medical supervision, and in addition St Mary's calls upon the services of leading surgeons and specialist in the region. Patients can be confident that they are receiving the very best treatment available, while the high ratio of nursing staff to patients ensures a high level of individual care; and the calm, peaceful atmosphere of St Mary's is in itself a great blessing and a help to patients in their return to physical, psychological and spiritual well-being.

Palliative and respite care is provided free of charge at the Frances Taylor Hospice Unit situated on the first floor of the hospital. Founded in September 1993 and named after Magdalen, or Frances, Taylor, founder of The Poor Servants of the Mother of God, the hospice is non-denominational and aims to help patients maintain their dignity, self respect and peace of mind in the face of an incurable illness, by providing relief from pain and symptoms, combined with support and counselling for both patients and their families.

Improvements and additions since that time are numerous; some of the most radical include a new boiler house, oil boiler and the ducting of running water to each room in 1950; a new lift in 1960, together with a new modern X-ray department with modern equipment including an image intensifier; new autoclaves and an incinerator, redecoration of the hospital and landscaping of the grounds, including laying out the car park, in 1970; and in 1980 a modern kitchen on the ground floor and a fully-equipped Recovery Room.

A subsequent major refurbishment scheme implemented in 1983 resulted in a fully modernised hospital with an automatic lift, two new, fully air-conditioned operating theatres, and updated X-ray equipment including a real-time scanner. Improved patient facilities now offered rooms with en suite shower or bath and toilet, a private telephone, radio, remote controlled colour television, and a nurse call system.

Outside St Mary's, The Poor Servants of the Mother of God continue to be active throughout the UK and in other parts of the world. The Order runs another hospital in Liverpool, student hostels in London, and homes for slow learners in both Liverpool and London. It also runs a hospital, a home for the elderly and a school in the USA, a training centre in Italy, and provides assistance to communities as diverse as the rural population of Kitui in Eastern Kenya and the street children of Venezula. The Order remains dedicated to the care of the needy throughout the world, and those who carry out its work are proud to be Members; just as its founder, who worked alongside Florence Nightingale in the Crimea, would have been proud of the good work still being carried today out by the Order which she began more than a century ago.

Today, St Mary's provides treatment for over 3,000 in-patients a year, offering high quality treatment at low cost to those seeking an alternative to the National Health Service. Continued investment in medical technology enables consultants to provide treatment within almost all medical and surgical specialities, as well as a range of out-patient treatments and diagnostic tests. The staff of around 200 consists of registered

Top left: *An operating theatre in the first half of the 20th Century.* ***Above:*** *The modern St Mary's Hospital.*

Learning to excel in beautiful surroundings

Few schools in the country have more attractive premises than those of Bristol's Redland High School for Girls, occupying as it does the beautiful 18th century mansion of Redland Court.

Redland Court, with its beautiful grounds and fine views over the city, has been the site of the school since 1885. Three years earlier the former minister of Clifton Down Congregational Church, the Reverend T G Rose, and the Reverend Urijah Thomas, minister of Redland Park Congregational Church, together with a group of citizens, had established the school in Redland Grove in order to provide a non-denomi-national education on public school lines for the girls of the Redland neighbourhood. The school started with just four pupils - who included Ada Rose and Enid Rose, the daughters of one of the founders.

Social and economic changes have influenced the development of the school. It has adapted successfully and continues to provide a broad and balanced education for the girls of Bristol. Challenges faced along the way include the war years, when staff and girls worked in harvest camps, gathering potatoes in the holidays; staff also adopted two refugees from Nazi Germany and paid for their education at Redland, and after the war an exchange visit on an annual basis was set up with the Elisabeth Schule in Marburg. On a sadder note, the tragic death of the Head Girl, Barbara Vickery, in an air raid in 1940, is commemorated by annual awards from the scholarship fund set up in her name. The school has also undergone administrative changes over the years, becoming a fully independent charitable trust when the direct grant status was abolished in 1976.

Today, Redland High School can accommodate some 700 pupils between the ages of 3 and 18. Its Nursery, Infant and Junior Schools are housed in three Victorian villas very close to the Senior School, where the secure, comfortable environment and the small class sizes create a stimulating, supportive, happy and secure atmosphere in which young children thrive, gain self-confidence and develop an enthusiasm to learn.

Above: *An early painting of Redlands Court.*
Below: *A modern day music class.*

While the handsome Queen Anne facade of the senior school has been preserved, many modern facilities have been added, including a superb ICT Centre scheduled to open in April 1999, a new suite of music studios, a sixth science laboratory, a magnificent computerised library, an excellent arts centre with an outdoor sculpture garden and a separate Sixth Form Centre with its own conference room. Additions planned for the future include a drama studio, and on-going investment in the very latest ICT equipment.

Redland offers a wide range of academic and extra-curricular opportunities, within the secure framework of a friendly environment which fosters the highest standards of achievement while at the same time encouraging the development of self-esteem, tolerance, a sense of responsibility, an eagerness to succeed, a clear set of values and a respect for others. Every student is given guidance and encouragement to develop their own particular skills, talents and interests, and this is reflected in the overall performance of the school in both its academic and extra-curricular activities. The examination success rate is extremely high, and a large proportion of the pupils go on to university. There is a strong tradition of excellence in music and drama, with pupils from Redland achieving great success at the Bristol Festival of Music and Drama each year. The Outdoor Pursuits Club offers plenty of challenging outdoor activities and events, including participation in the Duke of Edinburgh Award Scheme, and school sports clubs and teams give the girls opportunities to improve their physical skills and represent Redland in school matches. And in the Young Enterprise Scheme, designed to give young people experience of business, reaching the finals four times Redland's Young Enterprise Team is the only school team ever to have reached the national finals so often.

Today, more than a century after its foundation, the school continues to fulfil its original purpose admirably, with a continuous programme of development in line with the needs of the curriculum and a wide range of subjects at both GCSE and A level. A friendly, caring and purposeful community has developed, which offers a fine academic education and a wide range of opportunities. Former pupils in all walks of life retain happy memories of their schooldays, perhaps recalling particular features such as the enormous Christmas tree which stands in the school hall each year, covered in lights and decorated with the hundreds of intricate paper models made by the girls; but most of all they remember with affection the teachers who encouraged them to develop their talents, fulfil their potential and gain the values and qualifications needed for their chosen career, for creative leisure and for a complete life in society.

Top: *The Library today.*
Above left: *One of the school's younger classes.*

The heart of city centre shopping

The Broadmead area of Bristol has been part of the city's trade and retail centre since medieval times, when the main focus for market traders was the area known as Castle Street.

The adjacent Castle Park was once, as the name suggests, the site of Bristol Castle. This Norman-built castle was demolished by Act of Parliament in 1650, and very few traces are visible today. Remains do include part of the porch entrance to the King's Hall, a sally port, and pieces of the castle walls. The remains of a keep built by Robert, Earl of Gloucester, which used to stand above the great dungeon of the main castle, can also be seen. The keep dates from around 1120; Caen stone was used in its construction, and it is said to have had foundation walls 25 feet thick.

Following the demolition of Bristol Castle, several streets of shops and houses were built on the site, and the area became the main shopping focus of the city.

Above: Castle Street remained Bristol's main shopping area right up to the second world war, when German bombs hit the whole of the city centre area hard. While Castle Street was being rebuilt, the trade focus shifted to Broadmead, which then became, and remained, the central shopping area of the city.

The Castle Park area was cleared after the bombing and only the ruins of St Peter and St Mary le Port churches remained on the site, which was given over to parkland. The churches were left unattended for many years. It is only recently that the structures have been transformed, and lime trees, gardens and water features have been added. The Park also features work by internationally-acclaimed sculptor Kate Malone, who trained in Bristol.

Left: The 17th century Greyhound Hotel building, a former coaching inn and public house, is now the entrance to Greyhound Walk, part of The Galleries Shopping Centre.

Above: *The Galleries Shopping Centre was built during the late 1980s after the closure of Fairfax House in 1988; the Centre was opened in October 1991.*

Top left: *A view from the same angle as the wartime picture of busy Broadmead before the area was pedestrianised. A large section of the city's medieval town wall was demolished in the late 1950s to make way for the large Co-operative department store building, Fairfax house. During this time the Bentalls' building - then the Lewis' building - was also constructed on The Horsefair.*

Below: *Broadmead in the 1970s was already home to many of the retailers we see there today. Woolworth's occupied what is now the main entrance to The Galleries and has now moved back inside the shopping centre, but Thomas Cook, H Samuel and Dolcis Shoes still occupy the same sites.*

The River Frome, which had been redirected underneath Broadmead, is housed inside a specially-designed box culvert to prevent cellar flooding. The Galleries is now home to 108 retail and catering units and forms the heart of Bristol's city centre shopping.

Right: *This plaque details the history of The Almshouse within the Galleries development, now a café-bistro.*

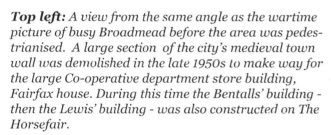

Fords - The ideas factory

World War Two brought about many changes in affecting the speed of development of machines and techniques and, above all, in the effects it had on people's lives. For two young men who enjoyed decent pre-war jobs with good prospects with the well known Bristol firm of J W Arrowsmith Ltd it changed every thing. Clifford Farrow, a print salesman at the London office, who had trained as a RAFVR pilot in his spare time during the air mad 1930s, was called up immediately. His senior, Leonard Shepherd, was Arrowsmith's sole commercial artist until called up to serve as RAF ground staff, the unglamorous, rarely decorated, essential front line personnel who kept the planes in the air.

During their absence Arrowsmiths were fortunate to escape the bomb damage that hit so much of Bristol while nearby rival printers A W Ford & Co were totally destroyed, the goodwill and salvaged stock being bought by Arrowsmiths. The owner, Richard Brown, wrote to his employees in uniform inviting them back as soon as they were demobilised while,

at the same time, he pressed the Air Ministry to release them as soon as possible. 'Shep' Shepherd had been redirected by the RAF to utilise his artistic talents in producing training posters in a department which had been evacuated to Harrogate. Here he was able to spend his free time in the hotel where he was billeted in producing designs for post war advertising material commissioned by forward thinking clients of Arrowsmiths.

After demobilisation Shep, in cooperation with Cliff, who, while working on research with the Ministry of Aircraft Production, had been taking a course in Advertising, and Richard Brown established 'an Ideas Factory' under the name Ford Advertising as a spin-off from Arrowsmiths. They were able to call on pre-war clients of the two printers who were eager to be front liners in the expected post war boom as war production plants were returned to peacetime manufacturing.

It was a revolutionary concept in marketing to design goods and advertising material, including packaging, all in one step by one team. The idea was mooted at the same time as another revolution was taking place in shops. No longer were customers shown goods taken from drawers or shelves by shop assistants who then wrapped their purchases for them. Shoppers browsed for clothing or hardware put on display or put foodstuffs from shelves into their baskets and paid as they left the new self

*Top: Mr A W Ford whose printworks gave its name to the post war design group. **Below:** Staff enjoying a Christmas party in the 1950s.*

strict deadlines and Fords have always prided themselves on being able to deliver the goods on time, which is crucial to the success of a product launch, advertising campaign or store opening.

service shops. It was soon discovered that apparently random displays of higher priced goods at the pay desk sold well to impulse buyers when attractively displayed on well designed stands.

The well trained Fords team has the experience and the strength to meet and to exceed customer expectations and to be leaders in their field.

By the 1950s and 60s international best names such as British Cussons toiletries, American Kelloggs, the cereal people, and the popular Polycell ceiling tiles used in the new craze for DIY home decoration were among the customers using Fords displays. The early display stands, like the photogenic Kodak girls found outside many chemists, were made of strong corrugated cardboard, this relatively short lived material has been replaced by more durable and permanent stands of wood, plastic and metal. Clients today include Peugeot cars, ICI's Dulux paints, Hewlett-Packard electronics and the Kickers fashion brand.

Top left and top right: *Past successful campaigns for Cussons.*
Right: *Martin Law, the current Chief Executive who was appointed in 1989.* ***Below:*** *Discovery House, home to the Ford Design Group since 1997.*

For a supplier to achieve such a client base it has to be good from every angle. Their liaison with clients has to show a keen understanding of their product and the market at which it is aimed. This expertise must be matched by inspired design which is right for the product and the ultimate buyer who wishes to associate with or emulate the image projected by the advertising. Fords have developed a talented and creative staff to keep them at the forefront of this demanding design discipline in a highly competitive environment. Production of the point of sales displays or of shop fascias is done to very

Printers of Bibles, accounts books and stationery

It was the connection with the former which saved the Lodge works from the flames during a wartime air raid, thanks to the influence of the Vicar in his capacity as an ARP (Air Raid Precaution) Warden. Around ninety years earlier Edwin Lodge, a teacher and scripture reader from Long Ashton, had moved to the West Street Post Office in East Bristol. The Royal Mail of the 1850s made its long distance journeys aboard the new steam trains but local post was transferred by horse, and even donkey, drawn vehicles. In addition to managing his sorting office and organising deliveries and collections Mr Lodge added to his government income by selling papers and stationery. He also dabbled in printing, all done by hand in those days.

Thus inspired his son John became an apprentice printer in 1867, first with Joseph Sharpe at 3/- (15p) a week, and from 1870, with the Bristol Printing Company who paid him 14/- (70p) a week in his final year. A remarkably generous wage! Six years later the qualified 'journeyman' printer had wed and moved into a house across West Street from his father. John Lodge printed the original articles for the new Bristol Rovers Football Club and Lodges continued the Rovers association for nearly a century. John's son Frank, born 1886, was also an apprentice printer for a fraction of his father's wage starting at a 'tanner' (6d or 2.5p) rising to 5s 6d a week seven years later.

Top: *The original premises of E Lodge.*
Left: *Young & Humphrys premises pictured in 1930.*
Below: *A caricature of Frank Lodge, 1908.*

out both the firm and their families by earning extra.

Wandsworth, a London council, turned to Lodges to make up the supplies unobtainable in the bomb torn capital and this contract enabled Lodges to obtain a larger paper ration for essential war work. Much wartime printing was done on automatic presses converted to hand power! During the Bristol 'Blitz' incendiary bombs set afire three adjoining buildings including an Amusement Arcade. The firemen, directed by the ARP Vicar, played their hoses on the printers of Bibles before the 'hall of sin' and so saved both stock and business.

1947 saw Lodges incorporated as a limited company which expanded under John William's management beyond the space available at the Old Market site. In 1966 he amalgamated with the Account Books specialists Young and Humphrys, established 1891, who had lost their Rupert Street premises to compulsory purchase. The new Company moved to premises in Jacob Street, where soon after, a serious fire occurred. Valiant efforts by staff ensured production was delayed by no more than two days. The 1990s saw YH&L acquire both WB Harris, short run colour printing specialists, and LF Hodges stationers to enhance the scope offered to customers great and small. The former includes Lloyds Bank, Imperial Tobacco and Dalgety Agriculture plus many smaller clients who appreciate service and quality at a fair price.

Top left: *Some of the staff pictured outside the factory in 1937.* ***Below:*** *Current Managing Director Douglas Lodge, right, with marketing manager Marko Oblyschuk.*

Frank joined his father's firm in 1908 as 'printer's devil', or odd job lad, and worked his way through to add to his skills until the call to arms came in 1914. He served, and survived, as a gunner to return home to take up life where he had left off. The growing company undertook general printing for local businesses plus a huge volume of work for Bristol Corporation and smaller, once independent, Rural District Councils in the locality. In those days the election printing contracts, which had been a mainstay of Lodge's occasional work, demanded that printers went around 'posting the bills' for the candidates. This was done aided by a pony and trap which was fortunate as the pony brought back the man who had to make duty visits to every pub on route!

Frank took control when his father died in 1932. The Depression years were difficult years for many and on Fridays a Lodge's man visited customers to collect debts in order to make up the wages for that week, Saturday morning was then a working day. In 1938 John William Lodge joined his father as a Day Release trainee until he and other young employees were called up into HM Forces during World War Two. Materials for non-essential work were as difficult to obtain as skilled labour and several Lodge men spent part of their military leave working as 'civvies' to help

Great Mills - going great!

The growth of the company has been achieved by working to a formula - though not one known to chemists in any laboratory. The Great Mills' trading secret is as old as success itself: to 'supply a wide range of top quality goods at the lowest possible prices'; in other words, to provide enjoyable shopping that is made easier for today's car-using customers by ample free parks and spacious, well designed stores. As these targets are difficult to achieve without totally rebuilding at least part of existing town centres,

From little acorns grow mighty oaks - and as the tree grows, a 500,000 times multiplication in size is not to be sneezed at! In 1972 the small firm of Clapton Building Supplies commenced trading with a staff of four in the Somerset village of Paulton not far from Radstock and Bath. In those far-off days before inflation (when Cotswold cottages could be bought for under £4,000!), turnover was a very satisfactory £50,000 pa. Today, Great Mills employs 3,500 people, and with an even more satisfactory income continues to spread its branches.

Top left: *The original site of 'Old Mills' where the name Great Mills originates.* ***Top right:*** *The Paulton Store site which opened in 1972, pictured in the mid 1970s with the Head Office based in the portakabin to the right of the warehouse.*
Below: *The grand re-opening of a Great Mills store by radio personality Tony Blackburn, in 1974.*

Mills DIY Superstores under the wing of RMC Homecare Ltd. Today the total has grown to over 90 superstores between Lands End and John of Groats, every one of them going from strength to strength.

In common with many companies of the nineties, Great Mills operates a Centralised Distribution Unit. This was first located at Avonmouth before moving, in 1997, to additional space at Severnside.
The company's commitment to efficient customer service ensures that 70 percent of all goods are delivered to all parts of England, Scotland and Wales. In line with its 25-year-old history of expansion, the company is constantly on the look out for new locations while the architects are continually planning their latest stores.

never mind the parking restrictions, Great Mills sets up shop in out of town locations. These permit parking for some 200 cars on average and the construction of vast areas of uninterrupted shopping space.

The next step from Paulton was taken in the first year by doubling and improving display space in the Clapton Building Supplies shop so that the DIY home owner could both see all the stock and obtain advice from the helpful owners and staff - quite a different concept from shopping with the traditional 'trade only' builders merchants. The deliciously overcrowded small town ironmongers, where goods hung from hooks in the ceilings and smelled of the accumulated stock of decades, were accustomed to a more leisurely way of working than the new generation of go-ahead home owners.

Clapton Building Supplies filled the gap by opening branches in Poole, Trowbridge and Exeter while turnover in the next five years leapt to £2,500,000. The enthusiastic team who had built their expanding empire were undaunted at the prospect of a three fold expansion by purchasing Monomart, a company in decline. Many would hesitate over such a risky step but with sound leadership and commercial skills the formula continued to work, keeping the newly named Great Mills ball rolling.

So successful was this still relatively small seven year old West Country enterprise of 14 stores that the giant RMC Group plc made an irresistible purchase offer in 1979. A year later the seven Regent Stores, based on the Five Towns of the Potteries, were acquired making a total 21 stores for the renamed Great

Great Mills pulls out all the stops in providing staff training and in-house promotion; how else would the firm have achieved its success? Their forward-looking policies led the company to pioneer the acceptance of NVQs (National Vocational Qualifications) among the retail trade, and they decided in 1994 to aim at the 'Investor in People' award, which would bring their methods and employee training into the public spotlight. In December 1996 the venture paid off...Great Mills won the award - and it was time to celebrate!

For a company to have grown from a small village hardware shop to a national chain of over 90 Superstores in a mere 27 years is an amazing achievement -'Great Going' indeed!

Top left: A typical store layout in the 1970s.
Below left: Garden centres have become a growing part of the business over recent years.
Below: The new store format.

Chard built and Bristol fashion

The Chard family of Knowle are as much known for adapting to circumstances as they are for the quality of their work and products. In the early 1900s the three sons of Mr Chard, John, Albert and Frank followed their father into the building trade. Chard Brothers has been painted in black on the grey company vehicles from the days when open topped electric trams ran in the streets of Bristol.

It was their skilled combination of traditional craft building methods with the latest in modern machinery which led to the development over a period of thirty years of the Chard reputation. Initially this grew in the then growing Wells Road area of Knowle where there was an inter-war demand for well built, stylish houses. Today estate agents advertise these houses as being Chard built knowing that local buyers will rush to buy homes that are better made than many others.

The Chard Brothers umbrella covered three diverse business enterprises each run independently. John, accompanied by sons Ben and Leo, stuck to the builder's last with a building operation run from a number of sites as his firm grew. Frank, and his daughter Violet, went into the haulage business which they ran together until 1972. Albert, the skilled carpenter, set up a commercial vehicle body building shop. In those pre-World War Two days customers could order timber framed car and lorry bodies made to their specifications

Right: Dick Gardiner ready for gas attack whilst working for Redcliffe Corporation Department in September 1939. Below: One of Chard Bros. trucks passing a trolley bus in 1928

of those who had done the grafting. This improvement was made in time to meet the enormous demand for ready mixed concrete delivered ready for use. By 1960 the company, strengthened by John's grandsons Tony, David and Bill, had become a flourishing engineering business specialising in the amazing machines which produce compost for mushroom growers. The 'White Queen' composter, as popular abroad as it is at home, shreds and mixes wetted straw and manure into clean, warm, moist compost in a matter of days rather than the months taken by nature. Another speciality of the firm is the making and repair of propeller shafts which link engines to axles, not for ships and boats, but for road vehicles.

for fitting onto the standard metal chassis, or base frames, that held the engine and wheels.

As this was, and remains, very much a family business it was natural for Albert to take on not only his sons, Norman and Clifford, but also his grandson Derek. The body building business has adapted to the times by concentrating as a body repair specialist operating in St Philips. John's building enterprise bought, in 1926, a former coal pit- head site in Feeder Road sandwiched between the coal powered power station built to utilise the local coal and Coles' 'bone-yard'. As the latter dealt with slaughter house waste at a period when public health authorities worked to simpler rules than today the smell of burning intestines and boiling bones impregnated the clothes and hair of everyone in the vicinity.

Chard Brothers lost their original base when Redcatch Road was re-developed as Knowle shopping precinct in 1972. Twenty years later the company again became homeless when the Feeder Road yard became part of the fly-over link road and Chards moved into temporary premises in the old Albert Road council yard. In 1997 they moved back to Feeder Road and built new buildings in a clear yard under the fly-over where they continue to maintain their fine reputation for 'Chard built and Bristol fashion'.

Top left: David Grant alongside a 'White Queen' composter in 1970. **Above:** The Redcatch Road offices and yard before redevelopment in 1973. **Below:** Chard's busy mechanised yard pictured in the 1990s.

The Feeder Road branch of Chards had been set up to produce lime putty and ash mortars for specialist uses. John and his sons established a small engineering business on spare ground at the site which dealt with local industries. The additional work involved the installation of machine plant for local firms who also called upon Chards for repairs to existing equipment. Following the outbreak of war in 1939 this department expanded and took on female machinists to replace men called up into the forces.

Post war re-development of civil construction was slow at first but a dozen hand filled mortar mills were in use by the 1950s. These were later replaced by automatic, self emptying mills to the relief

One of Bristol's oldest established Estate Agents

At one time Bertie Chappell and George Matthews were rivals; Bertie worked for Bristol estate agents Weeks & Sons and George was employed by a local competitor. Then in 1913 Bertie and George set up in business together. Chappell & Matthews' first premises were in Whiteladies Gate, in a row of shops abutting Clifton Down station, and here the two young men, assisted by their thirteen-year old office boy Leonard Brooks, proved adept at transacting sales and purchases of residential property for local customers. They stayed at these first premises until 1923, when they moved to the offices at 151 Whiteladies Road which the company still occupies today.

The company's first major expansion came at the end of the second world war; in 1945 they opened a second branch at 4 Redland Park. During the war the nature of the business had changed somewhat. Virtually no property was bought during the war years, due to the uncertain economic climate combined with the risk of bomb damage, and even after the war was over the ensuing recession meant that many families were not in a position to purchase. Instead, an increasing number of people rented accommodation. Suburban housing development programmes continued on a large scale, as the provision of decent housing was a priority; Chappell & Matthews was the main agent for a number of housing estates constructed at this time, including Westbury-on-Trym, Stoke Bishop and Henleaze, and much of this new housing was also rented to tenants, as purchasers were not forthcoming. Lettings developed into an important aspect of Chappell & Matthew's work, and have remained a significant part of their services ever since.

Chappell & Matthew has survived wars, recessions and a succession of crippling external controls and internal wrangling within the profession to become a strong and profitable company, acting as residential and commercial agents, auctioneers, property management and

lettings consultants, valuers and surveyors, being fully committed in all their dealings to the company motto of 'Courtesy, Integrity and Service'. The company has branches in Whiteladies Road, Clifton Village and Chew Magna, and handles properties in all parts of Bristol and the surrounding area, in all price categories.

The business passed from founders Bertie and George to their assistant Leonard Brooks and remained in his family until it was sold in 1988 to London and Manchester and subsequently in 1999 to Friends Provident. Leonard Brooks' grandson works at the Whiteladies Road office, his grandfather may well have been horrified by the degree of technology introduced by the third generation; rent cards, typewriters and his neat pen ledgers have given way to the latest computers, colour printers and digital cameras, with networking of the three offices, while Chappell & Matthews' website attracts enquiries from all over the world. The Bristol area can look forward to seeing more Chappell & Matthews branches open in the not-too-distant future, all offering the same high standard of service.

Above: *The firm's original premises in Whiteladies Gate.* ***Below:*** *...and today, the company's offices on Whiteladies Road.*

Not huge, but very good!

GF Mercer started work in the fruit trade before venturing out on his own in 1928 to sell fruit and vegetables in St Nicholas Market where he stayed for 25 years. For four years he ran his market stall on his own in the days when people enjoyed seasonal supplies of fresh, locally grown produce from the farms and market gardens within reach of Bristol. The railway company carried local produce to Bristol from the Vale of Evesham in neighbouring Worcestershire and also from Cornwall and Devon.

People then did not expect to eat out of season produce unless wealthy enough to run their own hot houses or to pay unrealistic prices. Except for South African apples and oranges foreign fruit and vegetables were rarely seen and, in general, considered inferior to home grown produce. In 1932 Ron, the first of G F Mercer's two sons, joined his father's business to be followed, in turn, by Ron's sons Allen, Stephen and Neil as the nation recovered from the Great Depression of 1929 and the early thirties.

Everyone turned their hand to whatever work had to be done from heaving one hundredweight (112lbs or 55kgs) sacks of potatoes and the 100lbs barrels of apples from Canada. Other vegetables and fruit were delivered in bushel sacks, nets and boxes, all of which were measured by volume giving a variable weight according to the crop. Once these had been stowed came the vital work of unpacking and displaying the goods to their best advantage to attract the eye of discerning and cost conscious buyers. In the wholesale business buyers expect that the unopened goods to be of equal quality to those on display.

The second world war was as difficult for middlemen as it was for housewives and caterers as all were subject to rigorous rationing. British farming expanded from its depressed dog and stick state of the interwar years to successfully providing the bulk of the food upon which we depended. Private cultivation of urban allotments rendered many families all but independent of greengrocers and their wholesalers as the nation worked overtime to feed itself. School children were given time off lessons to pick fruit from the grower's farm.

During the rationing which continued well into the 50s Mercers practically had to restart a business which had almost hibernated during the war years. The boom years of the 50s, 60s and 70s created a demand for new, exotic and foreign species of fruit and vegetables which Mercers met with imported produce. Some of this, such as the ever popular capsicums or peppers, is now produced by domestic growers. Today wholesalers can tap the warmer Mediterranean climatic zones found around the globe not to mention the greenhouses of the EU and the UK itself. Unfortunately as almost 50% of British orchards have disappeared in the face of French and Commonwealth competition some of our most tasty fruits are now endangered rare breeds!

The Mercers now have three generations of knowledge and expertise of their market which has expanded to include readily available cut flowers imported from Dutch and Channel Island growers to supplement the home grown supplies from the bulb fields of East Anglia and the appropriately named Holland area of Lincolnshire. Family policy is to avoid storing flowers so that trade buyers can pass to their retail customers fresh flowers in the peak of their condition.

Fruit and vegetables are today delivered in what ship shape Bristolians would regard as 'tiddly' little boxes weighing a mere 30lbs (13kgs), while the 28lb nets of sprouts can be thrown from hand to hand. Even the half hundredweight bags of potatoes can be easily slung onto a shoulder if there is no convenient fork lift truck to run a pallet load from place to place.

As always the Mercer family stake their sound reputation on satisfying their customers with first class quality and freshness of all their stock of fruit, flowers and vegetables.

Above: A redirected letter posted during the second world war. Below: Bristol's bustling flower market pictured during the 1950s.

A prime example of successful coatings

How true is the cliché 'the World is a small place'? Back in the early 1930s William Henry Payne was working for Shell Oil in Venezuela and met up with an American, who had spent his schooldays in the West Country of England. The two became a firm friends and before long William's new friend introduced him to an exciting new coating, metal spraying, in which he quickly became an expert.

Utilising the shipyard that had been operated by the Payne family for many years and determined to establish himself in industry, using his new found knowledge of metalspraying. He founded Bristol Metal Spraying and Welding Ltd soon after his return to Bristol in 1936. He updated many of the buildings and progressed to be the first company to introduce the process of metal spraying into this country.

The moneysaving versatility of the metalspraying process soon became sought after and within a year

BMS's rise to become the leading specialist in this field had begun.

As the company grew, funds were re-invested in new equipment - much of which had to be imported or specially made in this country - to satisfy an ever-growing demand for the 'new technology' coating.

As W H Payne's young family grew up and left school they began to join the company. His three eldest children, John, Peter and Beryl started work with BMS on leaving school. Sadly Peter (19) was killed in 1941 together with his friend Ron Horley when they went, in their tea break, to investigate an unexploded bomb which landed across the road. The bomb went off killing them both instantly.

With the outbreak of World War II BMS turned to supplying the war needs: torpedoes and exhaust systems for the aircraft industry were welded, blasted and metalsprayed.

A major customer was Bristol Aeroplane Company, who took over two of the sheds in Payne's Shipyard to store scrap metal for re-smelting. Fabrications and brackets

Top: *The founder of the company W H Payne.*
Below: *W H Payne standing behind a refurbished crankshaft.*

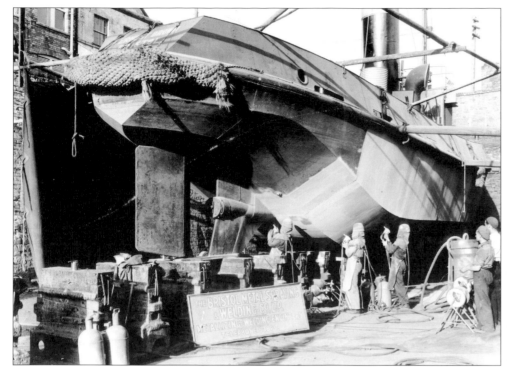

Stations and on of many of HMS surface ships.

The company continued to develop its skills and is today a leading industrial coating specialist whose capabilities include high technology and high efficiency coatings. Projects include coating works to the Clifton and Severn Suspension Bridges, Lords Cricket Ground, Palace of Westminster, Canary Wharf, Kew Gardens, Cardiff Crown Court, Marleybone Railway Station, Great Man Made River (Libya) and the engine components of Concorde, Harrier Jump Jets, Tornados and Euro Fighters.

In 1983 the youngest son Barrie bought out his sibling's interests in the company and took on full ownership. Sadly he died unexpectedly in April 1984 when his wife Gillian took over the running of the company with the help of the eldest daughter Melanie, later joined by the middle daughter, Debra. Today the team includes the youngest of the three, Victoria.

were made in their thousands for GEC and the company was kept working around the clock to repair the components for war production machines.

When the war ended in 1945 business was thriving, the company had over 120 employees and larger workshops were needed. Rebuilding of the factory commenced

BMS was re-named in the 1980s to accurately reflect its activities as a quality approved applicator of over 150 paints, resins and metal coatings for component reclamation and to protect against heat damage, corrosion erosion and abrasion. Today Bristol Metal Spraying & Protective Coatings Ltd continues to be successfully run by the family serving a wide market base including General Engineering, Plant and Printing, Aerospace, Power Generation, Marine, Formula One and Indy Racing, Oil and Gas Industries etc.

Who knows - it might just continue on to the fourth generation who have already started their education!

using second hand salvaged materials where possible. The power generating industry did not escape the neglect of the war years and BMS were invited by Portishead Power Station to help solve severe corrosion problems resulting from years of little or no maintenance. The main problem was the corrosion of the Tube Plates in the Condenser heads and BMS undertook a programme of trials to find a solution to the problem.

A completely new neoprene-based rubber coating, Limpetite eventually emerged and news of this remarkable new coating spread and eventually every Sea Water Cooled Power Station in the country was using Limpetite to coat and protect cooling water systems. Applications spread as far a field as Ireland and Italy. MOD approval was given to the product and Limpetite was used to coat the sea water inlets to all of the nuclear submarines and is still in use today in Power

Top left: The tug - Ernest Brown - being metal sprayed circa 1950. Left: A Heatric Heat Exchanger. Below: The current company Directors, Management and Sales Team.

Bristol Uniforms Limited - Protecting the World's Firefighters

Bristol Uniforms Limited is regarded as the most modern manufacturer of fire protective clothing in Europe today. With its radical new approach to information technology, and using the most up-to-date computer-aided design and cutting equipment, it has the capacity to design and produce fire protective clothing to meet virtually any specialist demand.

This company has a long history of remarkable achievements. John Gardiner, who founded the company almost 200 years ago, was himself a colourful character. He was High Sheriff of Bristol and also Postmaster between 1825 and 1832, and during the 1831 Bristol riots he was personally responsible for smuggling the post to Bath, driving a 'coach and four'. By trade he was a retail clothier, and he began manufacturing men's clothing in Broad Street in 1801. By the middle of the century the business had passed to his son, who continued to build up a brisk trade with the colonies. This export trade, instigated by Henry's father and already well-established by 1830, was further developed still further by wool merchant Charles Wathen who joined the firm in 1862. Charles Wathen was another man of action; reputed to have been capable of buying wool in the morning and having it turned into clothing by the afternoon, he ran the company for 25 years, was elected Mayor of Bristol six times, and his public services earned him a knighthood from Queen Victoria.

In 1899 the firm moved from Broad Lane to its site on Staple Hill, where it has remained ever since despite a disastrous fire which destroyed the original factory in 1921. Army uniforms became the firm's priority during the second world war, and efforts of the workforce received official recognition when the Dowager Queen Mother, Queen Mary, visited the factory in 1943. After the war the firm continued to specialise in uniform manufacture. The first fire protective suit was made in 1962, the year in which the company changed its name to Bristol Uniforms Limited.

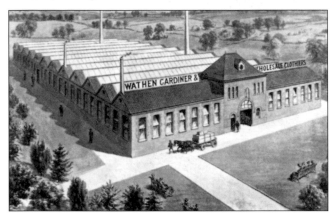

Since then the Bristol brand of firefighting clothing has achieved recognition worldwide as well as nationally; the company is supplier to 70 per cent of UK fire brigades, airport fire services, marine and aluminised firefighters, and exports to 86 countries including the USA, where it became the first non-American company to enter the market. With its position pre-eminence in the marketplace now assured, Bristol Uniforms Limited will carry on doing what it does best - 'protecting the world's firefighters'.

Top left: *The Company's original premises in Union Street, Bristol, 1810.* ***Above:*** *The Company's present site in Staple Hill, to where they moved in 1899.* ***Below:*** *The new London Fire Brigade Uniform.*

St Christopher's - preparing children to take their place in the world

A row of stately Victorian houses set in six acres of beautiful grounds and facing the Downs in Westbury Park provides the perfect setting for a remarkable school.

Specialist care and education within a stable and caring environment heads the agenda at St Christopher's, where the pupils, all of whom have severe learning difficulties, are given an exceptional opportunity to achieve as great a level of independence as is possible for them.

The school, founded on the principles of Austrian philosopher Dr Rudolf Steiner, came into being on 25th September 1945 when Miss Catherine Grace, with six children another teacher, took over a single room at The Friends' Meeting House in Redland. At first Miss Grace catered only for day pupils, but within two years, in response to the numbers of children travelling long distances, termly boarding was offered. Based successively in Thornbury House and Wraxall House, eventually a row of late Victorian houses, purchased as they came on the market, provided a permanent home for St Christopher's.

By the early 1960s St Christopher's had 60 day pupils and 60 boarders. In 1966 a new classroom block - Grace House - was added. The school's 21st birthday was a red letter day for the children, staff and parents alike when the Queen Mother declared Grace House officially open - and Miss Catherine Grace OBE was herself present at the occasion.

Today St Christopher's wide range of facilities provides for many crafts - and for swimming in the fine indoor pool. Computers offer the children an opportunity to learn and communicate, and the school's

many therapies include physio, speech and music. With a ratio of around two adults to one child, class groups number no more than six, and one-to-one support and 24-hour nursing care provide for their wellbeing. All proof of St Christopher's commitment to its pupils - who strive to overcome their difficulties and find their own place in the world.

Top left: The School Founder, Miss Catherine Grace. Above: Her Majesty The Queen Mother and Miss Grace at the official opening of Grace House in 1966. Below: Part of the School as it appears today.

This image was captured on 20th August 1938, when the days of Bristol's trams were very definitely numbered

Acknowledgments

Reece Winstone Archive

Local Studies section of Bristol Central Library.

Martyn Hunt

Thanks are also due to Peggy Burns who penned the editorial text, Margaret Wakefield and Mike Kirke for their copywriting skills